RELIGION AND SOCIETY

RELIGION AND PUBLIC LIFE

RELIGION AND SOCIETY

Additional books and e-books in this series can be found on Nova's website under the Series tab.

RELIGION AND SOCIETY

RELIGION AND PUBLIC LIFE

DAVID MUSKHELISHVILI
EDITOR

Copyright © 2021 by Nova Science Publishers, Inc.

All rights reserved. No part of this book may be reproduced, stored in a retrieval system or transmitted in any form or by any means: electronic, electrostatic, magnetic, tape, mechanical photocopying, recording or otherwise without the written permission of the Publisher.

We have partnered with Copyright Clearance Center to make it easy for you to obtain permissions to reuse content from this publication. Simply navigate to this publication's page on Nova's website and locate the "Get Permission" button below the title description. This button is linked directly to the title's permission page on copyright.com. Alternatively, you can visit copyright.com and search by title, ISBN, or ISSN.

For further questions about using the service on copyright.com, please contact:
Copyright Clearance Center
Phone: +1-(978) 750-8400   Fax: +1-(978) 750-4470   E-mail: info@copyright.com.

NOTICE TO THE READER

The Publisher has taken reasonable care in the preparation of this book, but makes no expressed or implied warranty of any kind and assumes no responsibility for any errors or omissions. No liability is assumed for incidental or consequential damages in connection with or arising out of information contained in this book. The Publisher shall not be liable for any special, consequential, or exemplary damages resulting, in whole or in part, from the readers' use of, or reliance upon, this material. Any parts of this book based on government reports are so indicated and copyright is claimed for those parts to the extent applicable to compilations of such works.

Independent verification should be sought for any data, advice or recommendations contained in this book. In addition, no responsibility is assumed by the Publisher for any injury and/or damage to persons or property arising from any methods, products, instructions, ideas or otherwise contained in this publication.

This publication is designed to provide accurate and authoritative information with regard to the subject matter covered herein. It is sold with the clear understanding that the Publisher is not engaged in rendering legal or any other professional services. If legal or any other expert assistance is required, the services of a competent person should be sought. FROM A DECLARATION OF PARTICIPANTS JOINTLY ADOPTED BY A COMMITTEE OF THE AMERICAN BAR ASSOCIATION AND A COMMITTEE OF PUBLISHERS.

Additional color graphics may be available in the e-book version of this book.

Library of Congress Cataloging-in-Publication Data

ISBN: 978-1-53618-904-9

Published by Nova Science Publishers, Inc. † New York

Contents

Preface ix

Opening Speeches xvii

Chapter 1   The Centenary of Restoration of the Autocephaly of the Apostolic Church of Georgia   1
Roin Metreveli

Chapter 2   True and Pseudo Secularism   11
Metropolitan Daniel (Datuashvili)

Chapter 3   The Structural Multidimensionality of the World View: Philosophical, Scientific, Religious, Empirical, and Artistic Components   19
Archimandrite Adam (Akhaladze)

Chapter 4   Science and the Medieval Christian Church of the West   27
Teimuraz Buadze

Chapter 5   The Key Presupposition of Liberal Theology   35
Daniel von Wachter

Chapter 6	The Coexistence Model of Religious and Secular Discourses: Saint Anthim the Iberian *Anastasia Zakariadze*	45
Chapter 7	The Problem of the Compatibility of Theological and Civil Subjects in Greek and Alexandrian Christian Schools *Avtandil Asatiani*	55
Chapter 8	Understanding the Phenomenon of Hierophany *Irakli Brachuli*	63
Chapter 9	The Canonical Foundations for the Restoration of the Georgian Church's Autocephaly *Eldar Bubulashvili*	73
Chapter 10	The Struggle for the Recognition and Acknowledgment of the Autocephaly of the Georgian Church – 20th Century *Tamar Meskhi*	87
Chapter 11	The Historical Mission of Svetitskhoveli and Georgia *Manana Gabashvili*	97
Chapter 12	Georgian and Foreign Written Sources on the Autocephaly of the Georgian Church in the 5th-12th Centuries *Levan Tkeshelashvili*	109
Chapter 13	The Restoration of the Autocephaly of the Georgian Church and Georgian Socio-Political Reality *Otar Janelidze*	119

Chapter 14	The Missionary Work of Catholicos-Patriarch of All Georgia, the Archbishop of Mtskheta-Tbilisi and Metropolitan Bishop of Bichvinta and Tskhum-Abkhazia, His Holiness and Beatitude Ilia II during the 40 Years of His Patriarchate *Metropolitan Nicholas (Pachuashvili) of Akhalkalaki and Kumurdo*	129
Chapter 15	Theological Education in Georgia During the Incumbency of His Holiness and Beatitude Ilia II, Catholicos-Patriarch of All Georgia *Protopresbyter Giorgi Zviadadze*	139
Chapter 16	His Holiness and Beatitude Catholicos-Patriarch of All Georgia Ilia II and the Multi-Confessional World *Sergo Vardosanidze*	147
Chapter 17	The 'Good Shepherd' and a Stubborn Parish *Alexander Daushvili*	153
About the Editor		165
Index		167

Preface

Liberal theologians believe in the necessity of a revision of Christian doctrine, trusting that science excludes the belief in divine intervention. However, divine intervention is perfectly in agreement with the laws of nature and science. Accordingly, there is no reason to reject the Bible and traditional Christian doctrine. A new model of the coexistence of religious and secular discourses is revealed in this collection.

Most of the existing papers focus on the problem of the relationship between church and state in the modern era. In this collection, different experiences are presented along with their significance for specific countries, mostly the Georgian experience on the issues of church and state relations. The role of the eligious leader in modern society is described, focusing on his spiritual mission in restoring, enhancing and developing traditional values in society. In particular, the role of His Holiness and Beatitude, the Catholicos-Patriarch of All Georgia, Ilia II is examined for his multifaceted endeavors to strengthen Georgian society and develop traditional spiritual values after the perennial atheism.

This collection is intended for readers interested in the problems of the main right of humanity, freedom of belief, in the modern global era and in the age of secularism.

Today, there is a lack of spirituality around the world. Traditional spiritual values are inhibited; in many European countries, the activity of church figures is stalled, and people are not allowed to choose education based on traditional values. This causes great dissatisfaction in society, as it is believed that traditional spiritual values are the main markers of national identity, and their development and preservation are essential.

Hence, this book will be of great interest for readers interested in the problems of spirituality in both Christian and non-Christian countries. It will be of interest for scholars, as well as for political figures who often encounter such problems in their activities.

Chapter 1 - The Georgian Apostolic Church has been an autocephalous church since the 5th century. For centuries, the Georgian Church and the Orthodox faith had played a major role in the consolidation and self-identification of the Georgian nation. When Russia abolished the Kingdom of Kartli-Kakheti in 1801 in gross violation of international law and annexed it by force, in 1811 the autocephaly of its church was also abolished. For a whole century, the Georgian people and its advanced intelligentsia fought for the restoration of the lost autocephaly. In February 1917 in Russia was the February Revolution, which created an objective basis for this. On October 1, 1917, the newly elected Catholicos-Patriarch Kirion II was enthroned. After the restoration of autocephaly, the Georgian Orthodox Church made great efforts to make Orthodox countries and churches acknowledge Georgian autocephaly. By the efforts of the Catholicos-Patriarch of Georgia Ilia II this was achieved and on January 23, 1990 the World Patriarch of Constantinople acknowledged the autocephaly of the Georgian Church and issued a document confirming this.

Chapter 2 - The etymology of the concept of secularism originates from the Latin word "secula", which means sickle. A sickle can cut fresh grass as well as weeds. Due to its initial meaning, secularism took the idea of emancipation from the negative influence of space. Authentic secularism is free from the burden of any kind of worldview. It frees the profane or secular space not from religiosity, but from such religious institutes that hinder the correct co-existence of the divine and the human. Christianity did not offer slavish religiosity to humankind, but a harmonious link or synergy of the divine and the human, the spiritual and the secular, the sacred and the profane on the basis of free choice. The synergic process is harmed by the illegal incursion of religious institutes into the profane as well as by the aggressive actions of political institutes in the sacral realm. Accordingly, secularism implies not only a defense of the profane realm from inappropriate religious institutions, but also an emancipation of the sacred realm from political pressures. When secularism preserves institutional boundaries, on one hand it facilitates societal agreement and peace, whereas on the other hand it creates healthy ground for a harmonious relationship and collaboration, or synergy between the spiritual and secular realms. Having institutionally regulated the sacred and profane realms over the past few centuries, true secularism was supplanted by pseudo secularism, a weapon for fighting religion with a non-religious worldview. The best representatives of the intellectual elite standing on the watch for world peace are conscious of the necessity of collaboration between religious and non-religious societal groups and they are searching for ways to return true institutional secularism to the world stage.

Chapter 3 - A world view cannot explain only one part of reality and neglect the other; just on the contrary, it should explain both the material and ideal aspects of reality. The authors set ourselves the goal of laying out the basic principles of their understanding of a world view, of a concept of its structural multidimensionality. In this paper the authors should also note, that they cannot agree with the classification of world views, when various kinds of world outlooks are singled out: philosophical, mythological, religious, every day, artistic etc. The authors' methodological approach implies the structural multidimensionality existing inside of a world view, i.e., a world view should have the possibility of forming such an impression on a particular phenomenon or noumenon thought out on the grounds of a synthesis of religious, philosophical, scientific, artistic, and experiential-empirical knowledge.

Chapter 4 - After the famous books of John William Draper and Andrew Dixon White (John William Draper, *A History of the Conflict between Religion and Science,* (1874), Andrew Dickson White, *A History of the Warfare of Science with Theology in Christendom,* (1896)), many researchers or people with scientist views think that during the Middle

Ages the Catholic Church hindered the development of science. This view is directly contradicted by the historical fact that the first universities, by the modern understanding of this word, had been originated in medieval Christian Europe and a modern scientific paradigm different from natural philosophy began to take shape at the abovementioned time and place. Christianity is a creationist type of monotheistic religion that teaches that God has created the universe out of nothing (ex nihilo) without coercion. Thus, unlike pantheistic religious-philosophical systems, Christianity argues that God and the universe are distinct from one another and that the processes going on are subjects not to purely theological principles and autonomous spiritual instances (Anism) but to God-created laws. Unlike Hinduism, Buddhism, Gnosticism and dualistic religions, Christianity teaches that the material world is not an illusion or a manifestation of an evil force, but a divine wisdom that the human mind is capable of perception by making observation on nature. This metaphysical environment led to the fact that modern science, as a socio-cultural phenomenon, was born in Christian Europe and not elsewhere, even though Europeans did not possess many scientific facts about other peoples in the era of the origin of science. With rare exceptions, the Church saw in scientists and science not opponents of the Christian faith but allies in the fight against the occultism.

Chapter 5 - A central claim of liberal theology is that miracles are incompatible with science. The most plausible version of this claim states that miracles are violations of the laws of nature. This paper argues that this is not true because the laws of nature describe not actual events and regularities of succession but forces. There is nothing in science that is incompatible with, or evidence against, the existence of miracles.

Chapter 6 - In the age of reason and knowledge St. Anthim aimed to base a new paradigm of Western Enlightenment on the teachings of the Apostolic Fathers. He entered a new field of discourse so that his communicative texts would be understandable and admissible to the epoch, relating a new system of values to a new sanctified style of life.

Chapter 7 - The school of Alexandria preferred Plato's methodology. The main problem for Alexandrian theology was the relationship between man and deity, which provided a rational basis for belief, while the method of teaching was considered to be an allegorical explanation of the Bible. The compatibility of theological and secular subjects in the Greco-Alexandrian Christian school is clearly evidenced by the work and views of Pantene, Clement of Alexandria and Origen, indicating a pluralistic direction of the Alexandrian Christian school. The pre-Christian school of Alexandria not only allowed the teaching of the seven free arts (trivium-quadrium), but also recognized their propaedeutic significance and full compatibility with the teaching of theological subjects.

Chapter 8 - "Hierophany" is a fundamental concept of the modern philosophy of myth and religion. The essence of this important phenomenon, more precisely, the concept regarding this phenomenon is explained as manifestation of the sacral and holy.

Chapter 9 - From the chapter a reader learns that Georgian secular and clerical figures permanently fought for the restoration of the autocephaly of the Georgian Church, which was illegally abolished by the Russian Tsar in the early 19th century. The result of their successful struggle was that on March 12 (25) 1917 the autocephaly of the Georgian Church was restored. The chapter gives us information on the basis of what ecclesiastical and canonical foundations the Georgian Church regained its independence. It is noteworthy that ecclesiastical freedom was soon followed by the restoration of statehood.

Chapter 10 - The leaders of the Georgian Orthodox Church took advantage of the state changes in Russia and on March 12, 1917, restored the autocephaly of the Georgian Church, which was illegally abolished by the Russian Church in 1811. In October of the same year, the Catholicos-Patriarch of All Georgia, Kirion II, informed the Orthodox Churches of Constantinople and other Eastern Churches (of Alexandria, Antioch, and Jerusalem) about this important event and asked for their support. Since the Georgian Church has not received any reply letters, the Georgian ecclesiastical and scientific community still holds the view that the restoration of the autocephaly of the Georgian Church has not been recognized by any of the Orthodox Churches. Research has shown that this view is incorrect. In November 1919, on the instructions of the Synod of the Church of Constantinople, Metropolitan Chrysanthos of Trabzon (later, 1938-1940, Archbishop of Greece) visited the Georgian Church. He presented an extensive report card to the Synod of the Church of Constantinople (published in the magazine Ἐκκλησιαστικὴ Ἀλήθεια, 1/8/1920). In the report card Metropolitan Chrysanthos of Trabzon had the request to the Church of Constantinople to have the role of conciliator between the Georgian and Russian churches in order to return to the Georgian Church the status it had a hundred years ago. Unfortunately, the Church of Constantinople failed to act as a mediator. Its inaction and silence, as well as of other Orthodox Churches, is explained not by ignoring the Georgian Church, but by the historical events that took place in the world caused by the First World War.

Chapter 11 - The historical mission of Svetitskhoveli is special. For centuries, it has played a major role in the religious, political, social and cultural life of the Georgian people. It is a landmark of correct values.

Chapter 12 - The Georgian Church is one of the oldest churches in the Apostolic Orthodox World. According to the old Georgian historical sources, granting autocephaly tu the Georgian church took place in the second half of the fifth century during the reign of the Georgian King Vakhtang Gorgasali. Considering the sources it can be concluded that in the second half of the fifth century there existed several bishops in Georgia mainly in large cities and religious centres. 11-th century Ephrem the Lesser (Minor) reports in one of his works that in the period of the Theophylactus of Antioch (744-750) several monks were sent from Georgia to Antioch.

Chapter 13 - The chapter discusses the attitude of the Georgian society and local political parties towards the restoration of the autocephaly of the Georgian Church, which was announced in Svetitskhoveli Cathedral in Mtskheta, on March 12, 1917. Among the political organizations in Georgia, the National Democrats were distinguished by the most respect for the Orthodox Church of the country. They fully understood the moral and religious, cultural or political significance of autocephaly of Georgia, participated in the fight for autocephaly and welcomed its acquisition with admiration. According to the party program, before the fall of the monarchy in Russia, the restoration of autocephaly was viewed with indifference by the Georgian Social Democrats (Mensheviks). Nevertheless, their leaders (Noe Jordania, Karlo Chkheidze, Irakli Tsereteli) supported the liberation of the Georgian Church from subordination to the Russian Synod. The restoration of the self-government of the Church was approved by the Georgian Socialist-Federalists, while the Georgian Bolsheviks rejected autocephaly altogether. Georgian periodicals have widely expressed their attitude towards autocephaly. The newspaper "Georgia" appeared as its defender, while the socialist newspapers "Ertoba," "Sakhalkho Sakme," "Alioni" and others demanded secularization and religion to proclaim as matter of conscience. A large part of the Georgian society perceived the autocephaly of the Church as a precondition for the political freedom and state independence of the country.

Chapter 14 - The chapter describes in detail the missionary work of the Catholicos-Patriarch of All Georgia, Archbishop of Mtskheta-Tbilisi and Metropolitan of Bichvinta and Tskhum-Abkhazia, His Holiness and Beatitude Ilia II during the 40 years of the Patriarchate. The past period for Georgia, as for other former Soviet republics, was an era of very complex historical changes and still remains so. The collapse of the atheistic empire struggling against God caused society to irreversibly strive for freedom from slavery and to move from godlessness to faith. At that time the Lord appointed the helmsman for all Georgia who has since been consistently leading believers to the Promised Land and he, a single man, changed all of Georgia - and not only Georgia - together with the Holy Synod and clergymen consecrated by him.

Chapter 15 - The chapter discusses the importance of theological education and its history, starting from the first and the second centuries to the later epoch. A special attention is paid to the most important Georgian educational centers based in Georgia and abroad, such as monasteries of South Georgia, those on Mount Sinai and Mount Athos, Gelati Academy, the Petritsoni Monastery and others. A special research has been done on how all this was reflected in the highly fruitful ecclesiastical and educational activity of His Holiness Ilia II which he carried out throughout many years.

Chapter 16 - In the chapter is shown the relation of the Georgian Orthodox Apostolic Church with the local Orthodox Churches, as well as with the leaders of different religious denominations for the last 40 years. In this context are discussed the meetings of the Catholicos-Patriarch Ilia II with the World Patriarch - Bartholomew and the leaders of the Roman Catholic Church: John-Paul II and Francis; also - interesting talks with the leaders of the Armenian Apostolic Church - Vazgen I, Garegin I and Garegin II; meetings with the spiritual leader of the Islamic Republic of Iran Ali Khamenei and the Chairman of the Council of Muslims of the Caucasus Sheikh Al ul Islam Allah Shukur Pasha-Zadeh as part of the Dialogue of Civilizations.

Chapter 17 - From this chapter a reader learns much about the 40-year priesthood period of the Catholicos-Patriarch of Georgia Ilia II, the long historical process of his relationship with the parish, his activity in the atheist state and the specific methods and means used by the Patriarch in the revival process of national consciousness and Christian values. Showing examples, the chapter proves that during a long period of history, when the parish demonstrated "stubbornness," did not listen to the wise admonition of the Catholicos-Patriarch and made a different choice (the tragedy of April 9, the war in Tbilisi, etc.), there happened irreparable mistakes, epoch-making flaws and shed blood in the history of Georgia. In recent years, when radical social changes, the civil war and Russian intervention have created serious problems for the parish of the Georgian Orthodox Church, the wise words and dispensation of His Holiness and his huge effort to strengthen the spiritual life of the parish, clearly leaves a positive mark on the spiritual and moral life of the Georgian population.

OPENING SPEECHES

PRESIDENT OF GEORGIA, MR. GIORGI MARGVELASHVILI

Your Eminence, the locum tenens of the Patriarch, Bishop Shio, Your Excellency Prime-Minister of Georgia Mr. Giorgi and Chairman of the Parliament Mr. Irakli, dear guests, I heartily welcome you today!

The present day, the topic of discussion and the spirit of your work are certainly significantly conditioned by a man whom we all particularly respect. Speaking on relations among the society, the church, religious movements, and the state, it should be noted that it was the Catholicos-Patriarch of Georgia who promoted the cooperation of the state, the church, and society with his life and work, who determined the content of this cooperation and possibilities of its implementation in a most difficult period; It was exactly the Catholicos-Patriarch, who by the grace of God, stood beside his nation and tried to help us to avoid the most complex challenges and admonished us on how to overcome this heavy situation in a most difficult period for our country when our civil systems were being destroyed, when economics, the system of established values were breaking apart. Accordingly, the spirit of today's meeting is mainly due to his merit, his selfless work. But let's take a look at the reality before which we stand. We will see that each of us as well as society as a whole, religious confessions, and the state face difficult challenges. When we have frank discussions, share our ideas on our problems, we see, that though everybody - different public groups, different churches, as well as the state itself - have their own way of development, there are issues on which we all agree, which are a subject of concern for each of us. I would like to tell you exactly about these issues.

First of all, there is a high level of aggression in our society, intolerance, a willingness to suppress, and in many cases even destroy another. For the most of society, as well as for the church and the state, it is important that our citizens not be focused on aggression and the destruction of others. It is also important that our citizens, often disoriented and with a collapsed system of values, not remain without hope, nor be in a situation where there will be no perspectives, but see the logical goal of his existence and life. Of course, this does not depend only on economic or living conditions. Spiritual hopelessness is much more complicated and, naturally, the church, as well as the main public groups and the state are called upon to facilitate the existence of citizens and help them see a goal and plan their future. Moreover, it is of great importance for all of us, that our society, our citizens would not lose creativity in this less aggressive, goal-oriented environment, and through their creativity, determine the welfare of their families, as well as that of society and the state. Although today we have common goals, unfortunately, we cannot always achieve the desired result. We often cannot change the aggressive environment to a more positive one. Very often disappointment, hopelessness, and a refusal to fight are often due to the fact that a person does not see the ultimate goal. All of this, in the end, weakens both our society and our state and church. That is why your present-day activity, your creative work is particularly significant for us, it is united by these values and plans to offer our society and citizens ways which would make their life better and more promising. I have repeatedly mentioned that I am particularly interested in Dionysius the Areopagite; I recently came across and got acquainted with the letter in which St. Dionysius discusses a very interesting, specific story, when a priest (I think it is a priest, I cannot tell exactly) who finds out that the archpriest of his church is unworthy, rushes to him, throws him out of the church, and takes his place. Dionysus sends this person a very concrete admonition in writing, in epistolary form. It is interesting how a philosopher of that time, a representative of the clergy, a man whose works actually determined a significant vector of the development of European civilization considers the question of this aggression, even if it is legitimate. St. Dionysius singles out two questions: the first that is the most important is respect for the hierarchy. He particularly accentuates it.

In the hierarchic order, even when one believes that he is right, when one protects holy things, he does not have the right of such an action hierarchically, as in destroying a hierarchy one destroys an order, which could be followed with infinite evil.

That is why he does not care how correctly the priest, Demophilus, assessed the archpriest's mistake. No, he says, no matter how wrong the archpriest is, he, Demophilus, does not have a right to do it from a hierarchical point of view, as he is below him in the hierarchic order. The next question which he discusses is the following: even in the case when you are right, remember that you should not remove from yourself and throw out someone who, in your opinion, does not act correctly. You must direct all your attempts and try to return him and give him the right to correct his sins or mistakes.

This letter written many centuries ago became somehow significant for me as, perhaps, the answer might be here as well. Hierarchy, respect for institutions, and not the destruction of the usual order, are some of the prerequisites for weakening aggression in society. When the main (basic) institutes are destroyed - and we, Georgians, have repeatedly witnessed this - destruction is followed not only by a loss of freedom, but also by those people who do not participate in this destruction being damaged significantly. And the second moment: society can never reject its citizen. Whether he is deluded or a criminal, he is still a member of our society, and society should make great efforts to return such people, and to strengthen the unity of our state.

This year marks the centenary of the next restoration of our country's independence, and it should be noted that Georgia has repeatedly managed to restore its independence throughout its history. Our ancestors created the first republic 100 years ago and created it in accordance with the highest standards, with the goals of a state oriented toward freedom. Your present activity is a significant contribution to the restoration of a free state, just as your work and thought of how to create a harmonious society are a precondition for the creation of a free society.

Thank you very much for uniting your efforts to achieve these lofty goals.

I would like to express my special gratitude to the man who devoted his life, his aspiration, and his activities just to these values. Many thanks to Catholicos-Patriarch of Georgia Ilia II for letting us speak on these issues so open and frankly. I wish you success in your work.

Prime Minister of Georgia, Mr. Giorgi Kvirikashvili

I would like to welcome you, Your Eminence Bishop Shio, Your Excellency Mr. President, Your Excellency Mr. Chairman of the Parliament, representatives of Holy Synod, Church representatives, representatives of the Government of Georgia, representatives of various religious confessions, dear guests.

It is a great honor for us that so many representatives of friendly countries have visited this conference. It is pleasant that such a truly representative international conference is dedicated to the centennial of the restoration of the autocephaly of the Georgian Orthodox Church. Generally, such a dialogue platform for the discussion and research of religious issues is very important, more over because the word and idea of Georgian theology have always been interesting for the Christian world. That is why I think it is quite natural that scientific conferences and discussions on such topical issues as "Religion and Social Life" are held in Georgia where there has been a rich experience of harmonious relations between religious and secular spheres for many centuries. This tradition and culture of relations founded on trust and respect between the church and society is one of the main achievements and the strongest support of our history. Georgian statehood is built upon it. Having always actively participated in the life of the nation and having been its consolidating force, the contribution of the Georgian Orthodox Church is immense.

The power of the Church, which has been a spiritual leader, moral support, and unifying power of the Georgian people for fifteen centuries, was the reason that the Empire attacked it, abolishing its autocephaly. Thus the Empire tried to weaken the Church, shake the strength of the nation, and cast doubt on national identity. Fortunately, our ancestors had great strength for a selfless struggle and this battle was crowned by the restoration of autocephaly 100 years ago, playing a crucial role for the national consciousness. Historical justice was restored through the restoration of the autocephaly of the Georgian church in 1917, we returned our Mother Church to the bosom in which our ancestors and spiritual fathers had been keeping religion for centuries and taking care of the values on which our country stands. It was followed by the announcement of Georgia as a democratic republic in 1918, and we celebrate its centennial anniversary this year.

That wonderful exhibition which Bishop David showed me when I came here is dedicated exactly to that rich and very complex history which we have undergone and we are all obliged to respect it.

As you know, Georgia has often faced severe trials and the Georgian Church, our Patriarchs, and Bishops have always played an outstanding role in such times.

In this respect, it is necessary to note the special contribution of His Holiness, Catholicos-Patriarch of Georgia Ilia II, our spiritual father who has led the Georgian Church for 40 years and whose merit before our motherland is invaluable. His wisdom and love win the favour and great respect of the peoples of all religions and nations not only in Georgia but all over the world. The fact that we have preserved and strengthened the historical tradition of the tolerance determining our respect for various religions and the peaceful coexistence of their representatives in the society is a merit of the Georgian Orthodox Church and personally of His Holiness, Catholicos-Patriarch of Georgia.

I am sure that today's conference will be successful and a thorough discussion of such urgent and important issues of our time as the relationship between religion and society will be held. I thank you once again and wish you a successful conference.

THE CHAIRMAN OF THE PARLIAMENT OF GEORGIA, MR. IRAKLI KOBAKHIDZE

I would like to greet all present, I express my respect to His Holiness and Beatitude, our Patriarch Ilia II, I bow down before his merit; I welcome the locum tenens of the Patriarch Bishop Shio, the members of the Holy Synod, I greet the President of Georgia, the Prime Minister, greetings to our esteemed guests.

Today we have gathered at a conference which is dedicated to one of the most distinguished and important dates in the history of Georgia, the 100th anniversary of the restoration of the autocephaly of the Georgian Orthodox Church. 100 years ago the liberation of the Georgian Church became a driving force for the fight for our independence and national freedom in the heaviest period for the Georgian nation. The church has always played a particular role in the history of Georgia. The clergy has always stood at the front line of fighting for our statehood and freedom. The fathers who fought side by side with civilians would appear during very difficult times for the country. They were leaders in the struggle, and that helped us to bring Georgia's independence and statehood to the present day.

Everybody remembers the history of Georgia and knows that Georgian kings united the Georgian state exactly around the Church and Christian values. Enemies of Georgia also knew it very well. That is why the attempts of encroaching upon the statehood of Georgia and breaking the back of the Georgian nation always started with fighting against the church. It happened so two centuries ago as well.

In 1811, the Emperor of Russia abolished the autocephaly of the Georgian Church, grossly violating the second canon of the Second Council of Constantinople. The nation had lived for 106 years without a spiritual leader - a Catholicos-Patriarch - and the Georgian Church was subordinate to the Russian Synod as a result of a violation of the canon.

The struggle for the autocephaly of the Church bore fruit only 106 years later. The Church of Georgia restored the autocephaly and chose Catholicos-Patriarch, St. Hieromartyr Kirion II, but the fight for the independence of the Church was not finished. For decades, the leaders of our church Ambrosi Khelaia, Kalistrate Tsintsadze, Melkisedek III, Ephrem II, and other holy fathers fought heroically against closing Georgian churches and monasteries, taking out holy things from the country, and the repressions of Georgian clergy conducted by the Soviet machine. Their merit before our nation and religion is invaluable. These people are national wealth and a special cause of national pride.

It was God's will that four decades ago His Holiness and Beatitude Ilia II became the head of the Georgian Church. Precisely as a result of the tireless work of the Catholicos-Patriarch of all Georgia Ilia II, the Ecumenical Patriarchate officially recognized the autocephaly of the Georgian church in 1990. The long struggle of our ancestors for the independence of the Church was finally crowned with victory.

A lot of things could be said about the merit of His Holiness and Beatitude, and it is well known not only to the Georgian people, but to the entire Christian world as well. His Holiness and Beatitude has proved with his life and work that the Georgian nation will never agree to yield up the most valuable thing to it - its religion; he has proved that fighting for the most sacred national goal always ends in victory. Because of this, I, like a Georgian and Orthodox Christian, would like to bow down to His Holiness and Beatitude.

We should remember that the history of the Georgian Church reflects the centuries-old history of the struggle and victory of our nation, and its deep knowledge is the duty of every citizen of Georgia. We should never forget about the sacrifices made by our ancestors, fathers, and public figures. Forgetting the past, we will never be able to create a better present and future.

We are happy that the heroes born from the bosom of our nation have brought to us the most sacred things from the depths of the centuries:

motherland, language, and religion. And we are happy that such heroes still live side by side with us.

We should always remember that the Church is the main bastion protecting national values, identity, and democratic values.

I would like once again to bow my head before every clergyman and civil person who has won one of the most difficult and vital battles in the history of our country.

I congratulate all of you on this most significant date, the 100th anniversary of the restoration of the autocephaly of the Georgian Apostolic Church. I wish you a successful conference.

THE INTERIM OF THE PATRIARCH, BISHOP SHIO

Your Excellency Mr. President, Your Excellency Mr. Prime-Minister, Your Excellency Mr. Chairmen of the Parliament, Your Eminence Bishops, dear ladies and gentlemen, congratulate you on this day!

Today we celebrate the centenary of the autocephaly of our Church. Autocephaly is one of the most significant conditions for the development of a church and a nation. When we talk about the relationship between religion and society, this implies, first of all, the realm of our thinking, the development of which is impossible without an independent church and autocephaly.

Of course, today we first of all think about the role and merit of His Holiness, Catholicos-Patriarch of all Georgia in the restoration of the autocephaly of our Church. We thank him. Unfortunately, he could not come today and I have the honor to congratulate you and bless all of you on his behalf.

One of the main topics is present day challenges, for example, how we should preserve a national consciousness and spiritual values in the era of globalization and post-modernism.

Mr. President has mentioned Dionysius the Areopagite and an attitude to a hierarchy. As you know, one of the main theses in today's postmodern philosophy is the rejection of hierarchy, since it is regarded as a certain kind of dictatorship; even when a person submits to his/her own mind, this is considered as a certain vertical value, that should be unacceptable as suppressing freedom. This is what a certain tendency of modern thought comes to, which, unfortunately, gains more and more power. One of the main themes of secularism is also the topic of desacralization, which today is also one of the most basic trends. Desacralization is considered a necessary condition in every public sphere, but our nation, in fact, is an idealistic nation in its thinking. The idea is always primary for our nation.

Our state and nation have been formed as a nation bearing the Christian values and, by the way, the thinking of our fellow citizens who are not Christians (I mean the followers of traditional religions) is also based on traditional values, and these are precisely the idealistic values.

ELMAR KUHN, EUROPEAN ACADEMY OF SCIENCE AND ARTS, WORLD RELIGIONS

Your Excellencies, Mr. President of Georgia, President of the Parliament, Prime Minister, Your Excellency the representative of His Holiness Ilia II, dear colleagues, ladies and gentlemen.

Let me give you these greetings in the name of our Academy President Felix Unger and my class "World Religions". We are honored to take part in this symposium celebrating the 100th anniversary of the autocephaly of the Georgian Apostolic Orthodox Church. It is also the 100th anniversary of the founding of Tbilisi State University. Both celebrations are linked together. So I congratulate you so much on the theme of this symposium "Religion and Science". It is really the best way to celebrate by strengthening the cooperation between religious and public life.

Deep down, religion and civil society are dedicated to spirituality and rationality. As the Byzantine Emperor Manuel II Palaiologos said about 800 years ago: *"To not act reasonably, to not act with the logos, is contrary to the nature of God."* We are committed to this logos so we may invite the stake holders of our religious and civil societies, the politicians, the educators, and all societal groups to take part in this dialogue of cultures, emotions, and rationality in order to build a society of peace and progress.

The key for the welfare, success, and peace of all is the knowledge of emotions, spirituality, and the economy. So the dialogue between religion and science has to be a general guideline for the prosperous future of our society.

Religion is also quite essential for the state constitution. As Paul Kirchhoff (professor of law and a former judge at the Federal Constitutional Court of Germany) postulates, every secular, legal order needs an unchangeable divine right as a basis for establishing an objective in the knowledge of good and evil. This should not be suspended by human logic. The state's religions guarantee that this cannot happen.

Therefore we at the European Academy of Science and Arts appreciate this celebration and symposium today. Georgia will provide an example of good governance influenced by spirituality and science in recognizing the role of churches and religions in civil society.

God bless the people of Georgia and all of you.

So, the modern tendencies imposing the ideology of desacralization on us, are undoubtedly pernicious for our nation. The main goal of today's conference is probably to think of how to overcome, comprehend, and oppose this - of course, on the grounds of our values.

I am very glad. God bless you!

I wish a great success to this conference; let it be a pledge of the following progress and victory of our nation.

GIORGI KVESITADZE, PRESIDENT OF GEORGIAN NATIONAL ACADEMY OF SCIENCE

I am quite sure that we all understand very well what a significant date we are celebrating. The centennial of the restoration of autocephaly is inferior in importance only to the date of the beginning of the history of our country. In this very difficult 70-year period which Georgia experienced, the Church, which had restored autocephaly, settled a lot of problems - it preserved the nation, identity, language, and many other things that are so characteristic for us. About a year ago, a well-known Russian scientist told me: You, Georgians, should at last admit that Soviet Russia gave you science and culture. I answered him immediately: You have no idea what you are saying, you are mistaken. This person was not bad about Georgia. What do you mean, he asked me. I answered, that culture in Georgia has a thousand-year history, and as for science, it has always developed in the Church. The Soviet Union banned the Church and therefore it would be wrong to begin the history of science from here. The Academy of Sciences has published a book describing that science has been developed in the Church and together with the Church in Georgia, and showing the reasons why the great Georgian public figures had carried out educational work not only in Georgia but nearly in all neighbouring countries, and even further abroad. The Church brought together and, it is even possible to say, saved the people during the last 100 years. Undoubtedly, our Patriarch, our beloved and incomparable Ilia II has greatly contributed to it. I would like to congratulate all of you on this remarkable day. I wish that we all celebrated this day and were happy not only because we are present at this event, but also because we are participating in it.

EMMANUEL E. GDOUTOS, ACADEMICIAN, ACADEMY OF ATHENS, SCHOOL OF ENGINEERING, DEMOCRITUS UNIVERSITY OF THRACE

Good morning distinguished guests, colleagues, and friends,

I am honored to come to Tbilisi and attend an international conference on "Religion and Public Life". As a member of the Academy of Athens, the most prestigious educational institution in Greece, I represent the President of the Academy, Professor Komadis, who due to his extensive obligations, cannot be present here. He expresses his thanks to the Excellency of the Ambassador of Georgia in Athens, Mr. Ioseb Nanobashvili, and to the organizing committee of the conference for their kind invitation and conveys his best wishes for a successful and productive conference.

I had an opportunity to meet His Excellency, the President of Georgia, and to attend his speech at the University of Athens during his visit to Greece last Thursday. Georgia is a country with profound cultural heritage. My first contact with famous Georgian scientists was during my studies at the National Technical University of Athens. I learned the complex variable method of the theory of elasticity from the classic book *Mathematical Elasticity* by Nikoloz Muskhelishvili, who comes from Georgia. He served as member of the National Academy of Sciences of Georgia and its first President during the period from 1941 to 1972.

Our two countries share many common cultural values based mainly on the ideas of Orthodox Christianity. The Church and the state in Greece go hand in hand. Our Church has a crucial role in the public life of Greece. Most of our national holidays coincide with church holidays. Thus, the celebration of our independence from the Ottoman Empire on March 25 coincides with the celebration of the feast of the Annunciation of the Theotokos. The state supports the Church financially: the salaries of the clergy come from the state.

Greece has suffered a great financial crisis in recent years. People do not trust the politicians. They believe the politicians have dragged the country into the financial crisis and austerity. At this crucial time the Church provides great help and stands by the needy.

Our two countries share common ideals and values. It is not by coincidence that in Greek mythology Jason, an ancient mythological hero, led the Argonauts to Colchis (on the modern Black Sea coast of Georgia) in the quest of the Golden Fleece. Georgia hosted Greeks during the period of their persecution by the Turks following the Greek defeat in Asia Minor in 1922.

In closing, I would like to express the willingness of the President of the Academy of Athens for a scientific collaboration between the Academy of Athens and the Georgian Academy of Sciences. I am sure that such collaboration will be beneficial for the scientific communities of both countries.

Thank you very much.

EYNULLA MADATLI, DEPUTY DIRECTOR FOR SCIENTIFIC AFFAIRS, INSTITUTE OF PHILOSOPHY, AZERBAIJAN NATIONAL ACADEMY OF SCIENCES

Dear Chairman and esteemed conference participants, It is a great honor for me to be here in the fraternal country of Georgia at this remarkable jubilee eventgreeting distinguished statesmen and heads of state, parliamentary leaders, respectable religious leaders, as well as renowned scientific, educational, and cultural figures.

I am here to represent the academician Akif Alizadeh, the President of the National Academy of Sciences of Azerbaijan, at this magnificent event dedicated to the 100th anniversary of restoration of the Georgian Apostolic Orthodox Church and the 80th anniversary of the birth of His Holiness Ilia II, the head of the Georgian Orthodox Church.On behalf of the President and the multidisciplinary scientific staff of our National Academy, I'd like to extend our warmest wishes of a healthy life, peace, prosperity, and happiness to His Holiness Ilia II and to the Georgian state and people.

Dear conferenceparticipants! Our peoplehave lived in close proximity andconstant contact for centuries. Beautiful Tbilisi and Georgia can be described as the homeland of Azerbaijanis too. Playing an important role in the political and cultural life of the Caucasus throughout all times, Tbilisialso had an important influence on the development of the socio-political thought, media, and culture in Azerbaijan in late nineteenth century and especially in the beginning of the twentieth century. Tbilisi was a political, administrative, and cultural center of the Caucasus during Tsarist Russia as well and it is noteworthy that the Azerbaijani Democratic Republic was also proclaimed here in Tbilisi on May28 in 1918. Indeed, the first head of the AzerbaijanDemocratic Republic, Fatali Khan Khoyski, and several political figures have been laid to resthere.After the occupation by Soviet Russia, the fates of the communist Prime Minister of Azerbaijan Nariman Narimanov, our great writer Mirza Fatali Akhundov, Abbasgulu

Bakikhanov, and some other distinguished personalities were also closely connected to this city.

After regaining our independence in 1991 after the collapse of the Soviet Union, new horizons for mutual cooperation between our states and peoples have been opened. It is worth mentioning that the late President Heydar Aliyev's policy of solid friendship and relations based on mutual benefit with Georgia is continued today by President Ilham Aliyev with the same steadfastness.

Dear participants! Today, Azerbaijan and Georgia are connected not just by oil and gas pipelinesor by railway lines, but by intimate bonds which have stood the test of centuries. For some countries of the world, the current close friendship of our states and our people can be seen as a great example of mutually beneficial good relations. The relations between our religious leaders and the close ties among our communities are also exemplary.

It has to be highlighted that as a result of the importance given to the consistent implementation of the policy of multiculturalismby the Azerbaijani government, Georgians living in our countrylive and co-exist peacefully with the Azerbaijanis and can practice their religion freely in their churches. The same is the case for the Azerbaijanis living in Georgia and their free access to mosques. Thus, it needs to be underlined that the religious communities in both countries contribute immensely to the peaceful co-existence and welfare of our people.

In general, I would like to draw the attention of valuable participants to the fact that Azerbaijan has always played a positive role among civilizations. Historically, it has always played a role as a geographic and cultural bridge between Asia and Europe, and from a political point of view in today's realities. Azerbaijan has been a country where representatives of different religions and nationalities have lived in an atmosphere of brotherhood. In all periods of history, the Azerbaijani people have shown the world an example of tolerance and acceptance towards other nationalities and religions.

Dear participants! At the end of my speech, once again I would like to emphasize that we are glad that the independent state of Georgia has achieved success today, and we want to see our neighbouring country as a developed and powerful state. I also wish the conference participants a productive and beneficial session.

In: Religion and Public Life
Editor: David Muskhelishvili
ISBN: 978-1-53618-904-9
© 2021 Nova Science Publishers, Inc.

Chapter 1

THE CENTENARY OF RESTORATION OF THE AUTOCEPHALY OF THE APOSTOLIC CHURCH OF GEORGIA

Roin Metreveli[*]

Academician, Vice-President of Georgian National Academy of Science. Tbilisi, Georgia

ABSTRACT

The Georgian Apostolic Church has been an autocephalous church since the 5th century. For centuries, the Georgian Church and the Orthodox faith had played a major role in the consolidation and self-identification of the Georgian nation. When Russia abolished the Kingdom of Kartli-Kakheti in 1801 in gross violation of international law and annexed it by force, in 1811 the autocephaly of its church was also abolished.

For a whole century, the Georgian people and its advanced intelligentsia fought for the restoration of the lost autocephaly. In February 1917 in Russia was the February Revolution, which created an objective basis for this. On October 1, 1917, the newly elected Catholicos-Patriarch Kirion II was enthroned.

---

[*] Corresponding Author's E-mail: roin.metreveli@science.org.ge.

After the restoration of autocephaly, the Georgian Orthodox Church made great efforts to make Orthodox countries and churches acknowledge Georgian autocephaly. By the efforts of the Catholicos-Patriarch of Georgia Ilia II this was achieved and on January 23, 1990 the World Patriarch of Constantinople acknowledged the autocephaly of the Georgian Church and issued a document confirming this.

Keywords: Georgia, Russia, Conquest, abolition of autocephaly, Kirion II, Ilia II, Catholicos-Patriarch, February revolution, restoration of autocephaly, national identity

The spread of Christianity from the first century and its announcement as a state religion from the first part of the fourth century favoured the consolidation and strengthening of the country, and the formation of the united Georgian nation. The adoption of Christianity as a state religion testified to Georgia's high level of development.[1]

The most significant step made by King Vakhtang Gorgasali in the sphere of the church was the establishment of the Catholicosate, thereby strengthening the independence of the country and increasing the influence of royal authority upon the church Vakhtang decided to invite Peter, a clergyman who was close to him, as a Catholicos. According to the request of the Georgian king, Peter, was consecrated as Catholicos by the Patriarch of Antioch, arrived in Kartli. Vakhtang Gorgasali founded episcopates in Akhiz (Klarjeti), Artaani (Erusheti), Tsunda (Javakheti), Manglisi, Bolnisi, Rustavi, Ninotsminda, Tcheremi, Cheleti, Khornabuji, Ujarma, and Agaraki (Khunani).

Thus, the Georgian Apostolic Church has been an autocephalous church and Catholicosate since the 5th century.

It is recognized in Georgian historiography that the cultural unity of the Georgian people had been strengthened in the 9th-10th centuries before feudal Georgia became politically united. This fact became a precondition for the unification of the separate kingdoms and principalities of Georgia.

---

[1] Essays of Georgian History, II, Tb., 1973, p. 64-76.

Of great importance was the fact that the Greek language[2] was replaced by the Georgian language in the Church. Giorgi Merchule presented a formula of cultural unity of Georgia in the Life of Grigol of Khandzta: the nation's unity with the church was conditioned by a linguistic unity as well.

Since the 9th century, the Georgian language has become the cultural language of literature, divine services, all directions of civil life and culture throughout Georgia. Giorgi Merchule declared loudly: "Kartli is reckoned to consist of those spacious lands in which church services are celebrated and all the prayers are said in the Georgian language". It should be noted that Giorgi Merchule does not imply only Iberia under the term "Kartli", but the whole country, Georgia.[3]

Georgia is a politically united country in the late 10th and early 11th centuries. The king of Georgia unites both Eastern and Western Georgia. The complete title of the kings of united Georgia is stated in the following way: The King of Abkhazs, Georgians, Rans, Kakhs, Armenians, Shirvansha, and Shahansha. Economic growth and cultural progress started in a country united politically.

At the beginning of the 11th century, the head of the Georgian church, received the title of Patriarch in addition to the title of Catholicos. Since then the Catholicos-Patriarchs have been at the head of the Apostolic Orthodox Church of Georgia.

Till the beginning of the 19th century Christianity and the Orthodox Church played a great role in the life of Georgia. After Georgia had lost political independence, the Russian government began to attack the Church. In 1801, the post of the Catholicos-Patriarch and the autocephaly of the Church of Georgia were abolished. The Georgian Church was transformed into the Exarchate of the Synod of the Russian Church. In 1814, the Patriarchate of West Georgia (Abkhazia) was abolished, and by the end of the 19th century all the South Caucasus, North Caucasus, and the eastern part of the Caspian Sea were subordinated to the Exarchate. The only aim of all this was the establishment of tsarism in Georgia.

---

[2] Under the influence of Byzantium, the Greek language was dominant in the Church, especially in Western Georgia.
[3] P. Ingorokva, Giorgi Merchule, Tb., 1959, p. 221.

The Georgian people fought for restoration of the autocephaly throughout the century. The outstanding public figures and clergymen of Georgia were involved in the battle.

In February 1917, revolution took place in Russia and the form and content of state administration changed. The Romanovs' imperial throne and the Empire itself were replaced by the people's government and the Russian republic was created. Georgian public figures, clergymen, and lay people took advantage of the situation and on March 12, 1917 convened a Church Council in Svetitskhoveli, Mtskheta, demanding the restoration of the autocephaly of the Orthodox Apostolic Church of Georgia. It was noted that the independence (autocephaly) of the Georgian Church was unjustly taken away, and at the same time the canonical autocephaly of the Georgian Church corresponded to the new form of the Russian government. The provisional government of the Georgian Orthodox Church was formed, with the chairman being Bishop Leonide Okropiridze (later Catholicos-Patriarch) of Guria-Odishi. It should be noted that the provisional government of Russia acknowledged the autocephaly of the Georgian Church (March 27, 1917).

On September 8-17, 1917, the Council of the Orthodox Apostolic Church was held in Sioni Cathedral, where the question of Catholicos-Patriarch's election was discussed. Two bishops took part in an election: Kirion Sadzaglishvili and Leonide Okropiridze. Bishop Kirion won by 11 votes. His enthronement as Catholicos-Patriarch of all Georgia occurred on October 1, 1917, on the city day of Mtskheta-Mtskhetoba.

Kirion had to defend the autocephaly of the Georgian Church first before the Holy Synod of Russia, then at the preliminary consultation of the All-Russian Church Assembly. He presented four reports:

1. The issue of the Georgian Church (historical and canonical grounds);
2. The causes of demanding the restoration of the autocephaly of the Georgian church;
3. Autocephaly granted to Iveria in the 11th century;
4. The issue of nationality in the Church.

The discussion ended in defeat. Kirion created a monograph *The Cultural Role of Iveria in the History of Russia*.

After his enthronement, Kirion actively began to work for achieving the recognition of the autocephaly of the Georgian Church on an international level. It should be noted that it was on January 26, 1918, on the day of the commemoration of Davit Aghmashenebeli, when Tbilisi University opened its doors, and Kirion conducted a solemn service at the University's church. On June 27, 1918, Kirion was found killed by a bullet in his own bed at Martkopi Monastery (the case was not investigated).

On October 24, 1918, Leonide Okropiridze was elected as a Catholicos-Patriarch of the Church of Georgia. It should be noted that the restoration of the autocephaly of the Georgian Orthodox Church was not recognized by the other Orthodox Churches. On December 29, 1917, a special letter was received from His Holiness Patriarch Tikhon of Moscow and All Russia considering the recognition of the autocephaly of the Georgian Church as a violation of church canons (canons 9, 13, and 16 adopted by the Council of Antioch), because of which the Russian Church severed ties with the Georgian Church. That continued until 1943.

On August 5, 1919, Catholicos-Patriarch Leonide sent a response to the Russian Patriarch in which he substantiated the illegitimacy of the abolition of autocephaly in 1811, but no results came of it. On June 11, 1921, Catholicos-Patriarch Leonide died from a plague epidemic, spread in Georgia at that time.

On September 15, 1921, a Church Council was held in Gelati Monastery, where Ambrosi (Khelaia), the Bishop of Sokhum-Chkondidi, was elected as a Catholicos-Patriarch. After February 25, 1921, Ambrosi Khelaia blatantly expressed discontent because of persecution of the Georgian Church, the restriction of the Georgian language, and giving away of Georgian lands. In 1922, Catholicos-Patriarch Ambrosi sent a special memorandum to the Genoa Conference.[4] The Patriarch demanded the withdrawal of the Red Army troops and holding of a referendum. He believed that the issues of the state structure of Georgia should be resolved

---

[4] The Genoa Conference was held from April 10 to May 19, 1922 and was devoted to the restoration of the economy of Central and Eastern Europe.

in accordance with the interests of the Georgian people. The conference did not consider the memorandum and, accordingly, there were no results. Ambrosi Khelaia was interrogated by the relevant bodies, was detained and, on September 19, 1924, the court sentenced him to 7 years, 9 months, and 23 days. Ambrosi concluded his final speech in court with the following words: "My soul belongs to God, the heart - to Georgia, and you can do whatever you want to do with my body". A few months later, Patriarch Ambrosi was released under an amnesty.[5] He died on March 29, 1927.

On June 21-27, 1927, the 4[th]Council of Georgian Church was held, where Christephore Tsitskishvili (Christephore III), the Metropolitan of Tskhum-Abkhazia, was elected as a Catholicos-Patriarch. During his patriarchate, the Church expressed its loyalty to the government, began to mention the government during the divine services, and some relations were established with the Committee of the Russian Patriarchate. Christephore III died on January 10, 1932. Metropolitan Kalistrate Tsintsadzeof Manglisi was consecrated as a Patriarch on June 21, 1932. His enthronement was held in Svetitskhoveli Cathedral, Mtskheta. He made a valuable contribution to the culture of the country helping the workers of culture.

It should be noted, that in October, 1943, Catholicos-Patriarch Kalistrate celebrated the Divine Liturgy in Sioni Cathedral together with the Bishop Antonof Stavropol and Pyatigorsk, sent by Russian Patriarch Sergiy.[6] This fact laid a basis for the restoration of amicable relations between the Georgian and Russian Churches. The Holy Synod of Russia adopted a decree on the recognition of the autocephaly of the Georgian Apostolic Orthodox Church. Eucharistic relations between the two Churches were restored. The decision of the Russian Synod is worth noting: "We recognize the prayerful and Eucharistic communication between two, Russian and Georgian, autocephalous sisterChurches, to our common joy, as restored... Ask His Holiness Catholicos-Patriarch of Georgia, having accepted the Orthodox Russian parishes in the Georgian

---

[5] M. Khutsishvili, S. Lekishvili, Again about the case of Ambrosi Khelaia, Mnatobi, 1989, p. 9.
[6] The Georgian Orthodox Church, Orthodox Encyclopedia, XIII, M., 2006, стр. 222 (in Russian).

SSR under his archpastoral patronage, to allow them to preserve in their liturgical and parish practice the orders and customs that they inherited from the Russian Church... and also to decide the church affairs of Orthodox Russian parishes in Armenia".[7]

On November 21, 1943, Patriarch Sergiy first mentioned the Catholicos-Patriarch of Georgia Kalistrate during the liturgy. It should be noted, that on November 7, 1942, Catholicos-Patriarch Kalistrate, the interim Russian Patriarch, Metropolitan Sergiy (later the Patriarch), and Metropolitan Nikolai (Yarushevich)of Kiev sent a celebratory congratulation on the 25th anniversary of October Revolutionto Joseph Stalin[8].

On April 5, 1952, Metropolitan Melkisedek Pkhaladzeof Urbnisi was elected as Catholicos-Patriarch of Georgia at the 9[th]Council of the Georgian Church in Sioni Cathedral. The enthronement was held on April 7 of the same year in Svetitskhoveli Cathedral, Mtskheta (on the Annunciation of the Most Holy Theotokos). The Georgian prayer service and Georgian church chant were restored in Sioni Cathedral during his Patriarchate.[9] Patriarch Melkisedek died on January 10, 1960.

On February 20, 1960, the 10[th]Council of the Georgian Church elected Ephrem II (Sidamonidze) as Catholicos-Patriarch. On his initiative, a theological school was opened in Mtskheta, which was transformed into a seminary[10] in 1963. The Apostolic Church of Georgia entered the Council of the World Churches during his Patriarchate. He died on April 7, 1972. On June 1, 1972, the 11[th]Council of the Georgian Church elected Davit VI (Devdariani) as a Patriarch of Georgia. The service in connection with his enthronement was held on July 2 in Svetitskhoveli Cathedral, Mtskheta.

On November 9, 1977, Catholicos-Patriarch Davit VI died.

The participation of Bishop Ilia of Shemokmedi in a meeting of representatives of world Orthodox Churches on the island of Rhodes (1964) is particularly notable. Here he raised the question of recognizing

---

[7] The Journal of the Moscow Patriarchate, M., № 3, 1944, Sergiy Starogorodskiy, the Patriarch of Moscow, Appeal to Orthodox Russians living in Georgia, p. 10
[8] Stalin and Kalistrate knew each other after seminary.
[9] Here church services were held in Russian for twenty years.
[10] It was named after Bishop Gabriel.

the autocephaly of the Apostolic Orthodox Church of Georgia worldwide. The point is that although the autocephaly of the Georgian Church was declared restored on March12 (25), 1917, no state recognized it (as mentioned above). The Russian Church recognized its independence only in 1943. But on an international level, neither Antioch, nor Jerusalem and Alexandria recognized the autocephaly of the Georgian Church. Some Churches (for example, Poland) recognized the autocephaly of the Georgian Church only de facto. It is interesting that only two clergymen from Georgia were invited to participate in the First Council of all Orthodox Churches. It meant that the Georgian Church was considered as autonomous and not autocephalous, otherwise three representatives of the country should have been invited. Also, in the calendar issued by the Church of Greece, the Orthodox Church of Georgia was mentioned as autonomous (subordinate to the Church of Constantinople). This question was not answered at the church councils and conferences of Belgrade and Geneva as well.

Thus, Ilia (Shiolashvili), on behalf of the Georgian Orthodox Church, having substantiated the legality of the autocephaly, raised the question of its acknowledgement on an international level with the utmost seriousness. When he did not achieve anything after scholarly substantiation, he resorted to an extreme measure - he left the council as a token of protest. It aroused great resonance. If the protest of the bishop forced the Ecumenical Patriarchate to think about the other side (we mean different state bodies of the time), he became an object of criticism. When Patriarch Ephrem II died in 1972, the question of electing a new Catholicos-Patriarch arose immediately. According to general opinion, including the Georgian flock, the Holy Synod, and society, the only candidate was 39-year-old Metropolitan Ilia (Shiolashvili), already recognized in the country, popular in society, thoroughly educated, and quite experienced for his age.

It should also be said that the government of the country unanimously recognized the candidacy of Ilia (Shiolashvili) for the See of the Catholicos-Patriarch of the Georgian Church (as a rule, the government authorities are always informed when making such decisions). But something unforeseen happened there.

The Department of Religious Affairs of the Council of Ministers of the Soviet Union and, in particular, its attorney, were against his election. The motive for the rejection was the protest of Ilia Shiolashvili at the meeting in Rhodes. Overcoming this obstacle became impossible then and the election of Metropolitan Ilia (Shiolashvili) was postponed for several years.

On December 25, 1977, His Holiness and Beatitude Ilia II was consecrated as Catholicos-Patriarch of all Georgia. Thus, 43-year-old Ilia II began to work with great energy.

Important steps made by Ilia II for the improvement of international relations should be particularly noted.

The Patriarch continued fighting for the autocephaly of the Georgian Church, which had started in the 60s of the last century. The heads of Orthodox Patriarchates of the world visited Georgia, among them the Patriarchs of Antioch, Constantinople, Alexandria, and Jerusalem. The Georgian Church restored the old traditional spiritual connection with Orthodox dioceses of the world through these relations, initiated by Catholicos-Patriarch Ilia II. In 1979, Ilia II visited the Patriarchate of Constantinople. He again raised the question of the autocephaly of the Georgian Orthodox Church and demanded that the matter be solved once and for all![11] The struggle yielded results: the world Patriarchates became convinced that the Georgian Church was true to its traditions and was capable of taking its rightful place in the Orthodox world.[12]

It took the Orthodox Apostolic Georgian Church 11 years of hard efforts to be recognized by the world as autocephalous. The question of the recognition of the autocephaly of the Georgian Church on the international level was considered on January 23, 1990, at the committee of the Holy Synod of the Constantinople (Ecumenical) Patriarchate. On March 4, 1990, Patriarch of Constantinople Dimitrios I handed a special charter to His Holiness and Beatitude Catholicos-Patriarch of all Georgia Ilia II, which confirmed the autocephaly of the Georgian Church.

---

[11] Cross of Vines, I, 1979, p. 79.
[12] The Catholicos-Patriarch of Georgia, Tb., 2000, p. 2017.

The Patriarchal See of Constantinople (which has the right to intervene in the demands of the Holy Churches of God, to show care, and meet these requirements) confirmed by the charter of the recognition of the autocephaly of the Georgian Orthodox Church, that the Holy and Orthodox Church within the borders of Georgia had received self-governance and free administration and, correspondingly, managerial organization since the oldest times. The Ecumenical Patriarchate recognized the Holy Georgian Church with the same structure and organization which it has had since ancient times.

Thus, the requirements of Catholicos-Patriarch, His Holiness and Beatitude Ilia II - to recognize the autocephaly of the Georgian Church since the 5thcentury; to confirm the title of Patriarch for the head of the Church since the 11thcentury - put to the Ecumenical Patriarchate by still in 1979 were actually confirmed and met in 1979. The Georgian Church has obtained real autocephaly as a result of the selfless struggle of Ilia II.

REFERENCES

Cross of Vines, I, 1979, p. 79.

Essays of Georgian History, II, Tbilisi, 1973, p. 64-76.

Ingorokva, P; *Giorgi Merchule*, Tbilisi, 1959, p. 221.

Khutsishvili, M; Lekishvili, S. *Again about the case of Ambrosi Khelaia, Mnatobi*, 1989, p. 9.

The Catholicos-Patriarch of Georgia, Tbilisi, 2000, p. 2017.

The Georgian Orthodox Church, *Orthodox Encyclopedia*, XIII, M., 2006, p. 222 (in Russian).

The Journal of the Moscow Patriarchate, M., № 3, 1944, Sergiy Starogorodskiy, the Patriarch of Moscow, Appeal to Orthodox Russians living in Georgia, p. 10

In: Religion and Public Life
Editor: David Muskhelishvili
ISBN: 978-1-53618-904-9
© 2021 Nova Science Publishers, Inc.

Chapter 2

TRUE AND PSEUDO SECULARISM

*Metropolitan Daniel (Datuashvili)**
Chiatura and Sachkhere. Tbilisi, Georgia

ABSTRACT

The etymology of the concept of secularism originates from the Latin word "secula", which means sickle. A sickle can cut fresh grass as well as weeds. Due to its initial meaning, secularism took the idea of emancipation from the negative influence of space. Authentic secularism is free from the burden of any kind of worldview. It frees the profane or secular space not from religiosity, but from such religious institutes that hinder the correct co-existence of the divine and the human.

Christianity did not offer slavish religiosity to humankind, but a harmonious link or synergy of the divine and the human, the spiritual and the secular, the sacred and the profane on the basis of free choice.

The synergic process is harmed by the illegal incursion of religious institutes into the profane as well as by the aggressive actions of political institutes in the sacral realm. Accordingly, secularism implies not only a defense of the profane realm from inappropriate religious institutions, but also an emancipation of the sacred realm from political pressures.

When secularism preserves institutional boundaries, on one hand it facilitates societal agreement and peace, whereas on the other hand it

---
* Corresponding Author's E-mail: logos.iccr@yahoo.com.

creates healthy ground for a harmonious relationship and collaboration, or synergy between the spiritual and secular realms.

Having institutionally regulated the sacred and profane realms over the past few centuries, true secularism was supplanted by pseudo secularism, a weapon for fighting religion with a non-religious worldview.

The best representatives of the intellectual elite standing on the watch for world peace are conscious of the necessity of collaboration between religious and non-religious societal groups and they are searching for ways to return true institutional secularism to the world stage.

Keywords: true secularism, pseudo secularism, synergy, mediator, the Catholicos-Patriarch of all Georgia

The etymology of the concept of secularism originates from the Latin word "secula", which means sickle. A sickle can cut fresh grass as well as weeds. Due to its initial meaning, secularism took the idea of emancipation from the negative influence of space. Authentic secularism is free from the burden of any kind of worldview. It frees the profane or secular space not from religiosity, but from such religious institutes that hinder the correct co-existence of the divine and the human.

A well-known 20th century Orthodox theologian, John Meyendorff writes in a chapter "The Secularization of the World - The Christian Idea": "One of the characteristic innovations of Christianity was that it was able to carry out the demystification, if you will, the secularization of the cosmos."

Pagan religion, which idolized various phenomena of the material universe, actually imprisoned the profane realm. By exposing idol-worship, the Christian worldview opened up a wide, creative playing field to the secular realm. The scientific and cultural achievements of modern civilization are the result of the secularization carried out by Christianity.

Christianity did not offer slavish religiosity to humankind, but a harmonious link or synergy of the divine and the human, the spiritual and the secular, the sacred and the profane on the basis of free choice.

This synergy was seriously hindered by the Roman Empire during the first centuries. Due to not having any rights and terrible persecution, the Church was restricted from acting freely in the secular realm. A high level of perfection was achieved by the synergistic process after the creation of Christian states, yet an aspiration for spiritual elevation along with victory was accompanied by defeat as well. There were some individual cases of the state pressuring the Church, and vice-versa. A view of the relationship between the spiritual and secular realms in the Christian world was conditioned by the replacement of monarchism with democracy. In the conditions of democratic governance having ideal neutrality, the old forms of religious institutes turned out to be unnatural.

The synergic process is harmed by the illegal incursion of religious institutes into the profane as well as by the aggressive actions of political institutes in the sacral realm. Accordingly, secularism implies not only a defense of the profane realm from inappropriate religious institutions, but also an emancipation of the sacred realm from political pressures.

When secularism preserves institutional boundaries, on one hand it facilitates societal agreement and peace, whereas on the other hand it creates healthy ground for a harmonious relationship and collaboration, or synergy between the spiritual and secular realms.

A definition of healthy, institutional secularism should be read from the Holy Scriptures. Our Lord Jesus Christ commands us to give to Caesar what is Caesar's and to God what is God's (Luke 20:25).

The spiritual and the material realms are joined together through human nature. When the public space is divided into the sacred and the profane, this carries a conditional character. Both spheres represent various aspects of a unified society. A study of their individual peculiarities helps bring about the unification of society and a harmonious existence.

True secularism prevents spiritual and secular institutions from having their roles mixed up, from mutual interference and pressure. The change of religious institutions during the transitional process to a democratic government in Christian countries was carried out precisely to the merit of true secularism.

A human being was declared as the measure of truth by the modern philosophy that has sprung up in the past centuries. Belief in the unlimited possibilities of the human mind, belief in humankind's independent freedom from God on Earth, and in the establishment of justice and universal prosperity appeared.

Religion was declared to be a private sphere of identity by modern philosophy and through this was a stimulus for the desacralization of the public space. Despite the recognition of a neutral worldview, modern philosophy's idea was turned into a tangible reality for desacralization by democratic state institutions.

Having institutionally regulated the sacred and profane realms over the past few centuries, true secularism was supplanted by a pseudo secularism, a weapon for fighting religion with a non-religious worldview.

Archpriest Alexander Schmemann, a well-known Orthodox theologian during the 1960s, wrote about secularism: "At this time, the entire world has become secular. In the best case it tells a person, 'If you want to believe but in no instance mix religion in any area of life - neither in science, art, politics, nor in agriculture. There is no place for religion here.' Regarding the fate of religion in this secular world where religion is not so much forbidden (because in the end, a ban of faith, prayer, and a personal relationship with God is impossible) as it is severed from every aspect of life, believers and non-believers must ponder on this. Why? The separation set as a foundation for secularism and which persecutes religion in the "private" realm, causes a person to become enslaved sooner or later and I add, it is such an enslavement where a non-believer is enslaved immeasurably more than a believer, because that which is called totalitarianism in modern language is a direct and inevitable result of secularism (A. Schmemann, *Religion and Society: Religion in the Public Space*)."

Pseudo secularism tries to come across with the halo of true secularism and make itself seem to be a servant to progress and humanism, but the character of its worldview brings about the opposite result. The banishment of religion from the public space by pseudo secularism gives rise to confrontation and polarization between societal groups. One of its most serious outcomes is a new form of religious fanaticism - the emergence of international terrorism.

Peter Ludwig Berger, a well-known American sociologist and one of the apologists for secularism in the past, writes in his book *The Social Construction of Reality: A Treatise in the Sociology of Knowledge* (1996): "Whoever denies the importance of religion when analyzing modern relationships, they do so because of their own fear and risk." On November 14, 2001, Jürgen Habermas, a German philosopher, stated when being awarded the Peace Prize: "The secular majority must not make decisions on important issues until it listens to its opponent who feels themselves to have been deprived of their rights by the majority due to their religious faith."

In the book *The Dialectics of Secularization* he expounds upon the idea that the propagation of a secular worldview towards every person by the government is incompatible with the ideal neutrality of the state, because it cannot guarantee equal, ethical freedom for every citizen. He concludes on the basis of this idea:

"Non-religious people, as far as they are citizens of a state, must not deny a religious perception of the world in the potentiality of truth in principle and they must not take away religious people's rights to make their own contribution to a societal discussion through the means of religious concepts."

In 2012 at a conference dedicated to the 35th anniversary of His Holiness Ilia II's enthronization, the same thought regarding secularism was expressed by Mr. David Usupashvili, the Speaker of Parliament at that time: "An erroneous conclusion is being made, as if a liberal democracy implies secularization between religion and the state on a worldview level. In reality, secularization is at the institutional level. The secularization of religion and the state at the worldview level is the beginning of a new totalitarianism, an inevitable beginning."

The best representatives of the intellectual elite standing on the watch for world peace are conscious of the necessity of collaboration between religious and non-religious societal groups and they are searching for ways to return true institutional secularism to the world stage.

Modern philosophy differentiates the two principal currents in the history of human civilization: Eastern and Western. The primacy of the heart and intuition in Eastern culture, whereas that of the mind and the intellect in Western culture is apparent. A mutual enrichment by these two currents represents the main motivating power for the world's harmonious development.

Love without wisdom is blind, whereas wisdom without love is vanity. A deficit of healthy thought gives birth to religious fanaticism, whereas a cooling of the heart - anti-religious radicalism.

Having many centuries of a tradition of a dialogue between civilizations, Georgia might fulfill the role of cultural mediator between eastern and western, as well as between southern and northern countries. The role of the Georgian Church and its leaders was always distinguished in carrying out this kind of dialogue.

Today, Catholicos-Patriarch Ilia II of all Georgia is one of the leaders and facilitators of the dialogue between civilizations. The pacificist nature characteristic of our national identity was especially manifested during his 40-year patriarchate within the country as well as abroad.

Catholicos-Patriarch Ilia II of Georgia states: "We are living in a time filled with contradictions, complex processes are taking place all throughout the world. On one hand, great steps are being taken in science and technology, but in light of spirituality there is obviously some regression. Humanity has become defenseless before our eyes in a very short period, humans have become even more cold-hearted and indifferent towards the pain of others. Sin however has flourished and become legalized. ...Until governments become aware of the importance of faith in God and assist in instilling this faith within society, the situation will not be rectified." (Patriarchal Announcements, 2016)

Being at a critical juncture, we express hope that the modern world will overcome the obstacles facing it through the unification of spiritual and physical forces and embark on a road of peace.

REFERENCES

Jürgen Habermas. (2007). *The Dialectics of Secularization: On Reason and Religion.*
Peter L. Berger. (1996). *Secularism in Retreat.*
Prot. Alexander Schmemann. *Conversations on Radio Liberty*, Russia.
Protopresbyter John Meyendorf (2004). *Proof of Orthodoxy in the Modern World*, Russia, Moscow.

In: Religion and Public Life
Editor: David Muskhelishvili
ISBN: 978-1-53618-904-9
© 2021 Nova Science Publishers, Inc.

Chapter 3

THE STRUCTURAL MULTIDIMENSIONALITY OF THE WORLD VIEW: PHILOSOPHICAL, SCIENTIFIC, RELIGIOUS, EMPIRICAL, AND ARTISTIC COMPONENTS

Archimandrite Adam (Akhaladze)[*]
Rector of Saint King Tamar University of the Georgian Patriarchate,
Tbilisi, Georgia

ABSTRACT

A world view cannot explain only one part of reality and neglect the other; just on the contrary, it should explain both the material and ideal aspects of reality. We set ourselves the goal of laying out the basic principles of our understanding of a world view, of a concept of its structural multidimensionality.

In this paper we should also note, that we cannot agree with the classification of world views, when various kinds of world outlooks are singled out: philosophical, mythological, religious, every day, artistic etc. Our methodological approach implies the structural multidimensionality existing inside of a world view, i.e., a world view should have the

---

[*] Corresponding Author E-mail: adam.vakh@gmail.com.

possibility of forming such an impression on a particular phenomenon or noumenon thought out on the grounds of a synthesis of religious, philosophical, scientific, artistic, and experiential-empirical knowledge.

Keywords: world view, structural multidimensionality, faith, knowledge, phenomenon, noumenon, reality

> "Knowledge and faith are not an end in themselves but a path leading to truth and God." Ilia II, Catholicos-Patriarch of all Georgia

Knowledge and faith are fundamental categories on a path, uneven and full of obstacles, of becoming cognizant of the truth. Our world view defines both the character and results of this path. That is why we set ourselves the goal of laying out the foundations (basic principles) of our understanding of a world view, of a concept of its structural multidimensionality.

The definition of these two very important concepts - faith and knowledge - their transdisciplinary comprehension and comparison, and the study of their interrelations are intellectual processes of an ideological nature. That means that the reflection, academic study, and scientific research of the aforementioned issues should be conducted in such a way, that all the questions be answered like we answer questions relating to the existence, life and activity of a man - his biological, social, cultural, and spiritual being - as well as the place set for him in the universe and an understanding of his predestination. After all, a world view defines the essence, character, order, purposefulness, and content of a man's activity. Whatever our self and its position are, the same is our perception of the world.

When we discuss the spiritual, moral, and philosophical essences of phenomena, as well as noumena, the weakness of the "lonely" mind to comprehend the ethical dilemmas facing politics, modern technologies, biomedicine, global economics, and ecology becomes clear, which is not enough without faith, a philosophical discourse, and a projection into an artistic space.

It must be said, that the issue of the interrelation of faith and knowledge has had a particular fate in the history of mankind.

There have always been different points of view on this issue. Now it has become inevitable as faith and knowledge have permanently been opposed. Tertullian brought light to this division, when he asked the question: "What is common between Athens and Jerusalem?" Philosophy for him was antagonistic to Christianity. Augustine and Anselm also were adherents of this tradition. It is interesting that reason prevailed in Islamic culture. Avicenna and Averroes (Ibn Rushdi) claimed in the Middle Ages that reason leads us to the absolute truth, and faith is a short way for those who are not endowed with special mental talents. As for Thomas of Aquinas, he maintained that both faith and reason lead us to the truth, though he considered that one and the same person cannot believe and rationally comprehend the truth at the same time. Thus, Thomas' doctrine separates knowledge and faith from each other and creates the basis for their opposition.

We have not been able to bypass this historical review, and now we would like to note that attempts to stand only on the side of faith or of knowledge have still been continued, as a result of which there are repeated failures in the analysis and evaluation of this very important issue.

Let us recall that the issue of the interrelationship of knowledge and faith was raised in a new way in the philosophy of the 20th century, which was uniquely resolved in favour of the complete primacy of knowledge in Marxist ideology. Religious faith was favoured neither by the National Socialists, nor by the Social Democrats, nor by the majority of bourgeois ideologists.

The opinion on the nature of science was fundamentally changed in the West in the 20th century: not only the Marxist dialectic-materialistic theory of reflection was rejected, but even eternity and the stability of scientific laws.

Moreover: in studying the subject, the classical type of scientific rationality rejected everything that was associated with the subject of cognition, man, and scientist. The universe of evaluation and values was repudiated from science. This situation was changed only in the

20th century, when it was acknowledged how deeply and extensively the human, i.e., the subjective, universe, was woven into the morphological and functional structures of science.

As science abandoned those old claims that only it was the true reflector of reality, religious faith (as well as philosophy and art) returned to the place they had once received through Kant's attempts. It became possible to have an equal dialogue between representatives of science and religion, the aim of which is the development of a right world view.

As we see, the limits of assessing the interrelation of faith and knowledge, as a manifestation of a certain world view, exceed the limits of scientific discussion.

Although, science, on the one hand, and philosophical, religious, artistic thought, on the other, essentially differ from each other and even represent two poles of modern culture, there is no insurmountable border between them. Just on the contrary, there is a prop in their nature, on which the tendencies of their rapprochement arose. The same thing took place in the creative work of Ilia the Righteous (Chavchavadze), F. Dostoevsky, Luka Voyno-Yasenetsky, Bishop Gabriel, Alfred Whitehead, and many others.

Thus, the question of what is a world view, what is its make-up or varieties, and laws of existence, is important, because it defines the character of our discussion, dialogue, polylogue, discussion, or discourse.

If we had started from the beginning, we would have raised the question: What is a world view?

A world view is a fundamental cognitive orientation of an individual or society, which comprises knowledge on the universe and on a man's place in it - the ideas, evaluations, artistic imaginations, relations with the outer world and himself, as well as life positions, creed, ideals, principles of cognition and activity, and value-hierarchical attitude conditioned by these ideas.

Today, philosophers single out the following components of a world view:

1. Knowledge: the main component of any world view; the wider the field of knowledge, the more reasonable and thoughtful is a person's life

position; 2. Feelings (emotions); 3 Values: their perception happens in light of understanding of our own aims, requirements, interests, the meaning of life; 4. Behaviour - practical, behavioral manifestations of our own ideas and opinions; 5. Creed - the unity of knowledge and will comprising personal and public opinions, which is accepted by other people either with doubt or without it. Creed is a driving force of the masses and, at the same time, a life leaven of the people with especially firm ideological principles; 6. Character is a unity of personal features, which assists in the development and formation of a world view; the spheres of manifestation of character are: a) will (the ability of well thought out independent activity), b) faith (comprises the attitude towards one's self and other people; religious faith is not implied here) and c) suspicion (being critical, proceeding from knowledge and values).

Comprehending these components is necessary when discussing the issues given below.

We have already said that the goal of the dialogue should be the development of a right world view. What is implied in "right"? This question is logical, more so that we all live or should live in a multicultural and pluralistic society.

A right world view does not mean at all to dictate the primacy of a world outlook, or - God forbid, that we thought so - perfection! No, it means a methodologically sound world view.

After all, a world view determines the thought of an individual and society, their social and psychological attitudes. A free society chooses an active public position, but a society adapted to slavery - a passive one.

The more a world view encompasses, the wider a horizon of the perception of reality and the freer the human consciousness are, the larger and more global categories such a society thinks about and breathes. And if a society's horizon of thought is replaced by the confines of personal life and interests, it points at tendencies oriented more towards slavery.

Both a free individual and a free society striving to spiritual perfection possess the power to think on the scales of a country, planet, and the universe! If such people are in a country, if different groups of a society breathe in this way, such a country and nation (people) will have a great future - it will fulfill both its historical and spiritual missions!

Thus, a world view cannot explain only one part of reality and neglect the other; just on the contrary, it should explain both the material and ideal aspects of reality.

A world view is a multidimensional category. We have isolated the religious, philosophical, scientific, empirical, and artistic dimensions. A so-called right world view should "work" in all dimensions, i.e., it should give a possibility to discuss any phenomenon or noumenon in each of these dimensions, as, otherwise, the fewer dimensions a world view discourse is comprised of, the more incomplete our view will be.

We should also note here, that we cannot agree with the classification of world views, when various kinds of world outlooks are singled out: philosophical, mythological, religious, every day, artistic etc. Our methodological approach implies the structural multidimensionality existing inside of a world view, i.e., a world view should have the possibility of forming such an impression on a particular phenomenon or noumenon thought out on the grounds of a synthesis of religious, philosophical, scientific, artistic, and experiential-empirical knowledge.

If a world view "works" only in one dimension, it is not perfect, as in such a case the universe could be considered from positions of only a religious or scientific world view, and existence - based only on an empirical or artistic world view. But, after all, a man exists and works in one whole reality and not in two different realities. A world view should comprise both cosmological (about the surrounding universe) and anthropological (such as psychological, metapsychological, social, cultural, religious, etc.) dimensions.

REFERENCES

Archimandrite Adam (Vakhtang Akhaladze), Jerusalem and Athens (Religion and Science: Attempts of Integration), *Journal of Gelati Academy of Sciences,* 2007, N3, pp. 10-28.

Archimandrite Adam (Vakhtang Akhaladze), *Questions of the Interrelation of Faith and Knowledge in the Epistles of Ilia II, Catholicos-Patriarch of all Georgia, Religion,* 2002, NN 10-11-12, pp. 13-23.

Archimandrite Adam (Vakhtang Akhaladze), Saint King Tamar University of the Georgian Patriarchate, National and International Dimensions of Culture, Education and Health Care, International Week 2018, "Science in Motion", 11th - 15th of June, Abstracts, Catholic University of Applied Sciences, Freiburg, Germany, 2018. – pp. 15-16.

Archimandrite Adam (Vakhtang Akhaladze), The Harmonization of Faith and Knowledge: A Cultural Context, *The Third International Scientific Conference "Science and Religion",* Tbilisi, 4-5 November, 2014, pp. 80-81.

Archimandrite Adam (Vakhtang Akhaladze), The Possibilities of the Integration of Religious and Scientific World Views in Fundamental Bioethics, *Journal of Gelati Academy of Sciences,* 2003. N10, pp. 23-55.

Ilia the Second (Gudushauri-Shiolashvili), *Catholicos-Patriarch of all Georgia, Epistles, Speeches, Sermons,* Vol. I, Publishing House of the Georgian Patriarchate, Tbilisi, 1997, p. 296.

Lipe, D. L. *Faith and Knowledge.* - https://www.apologeticspress.org/rr/reprints/Faith-and-Knowledge.pdf. - May 11, 2018.

Welton M. *Jurgen Habermas on "Faith and Knowledge".* - https://www.counterpunch.org/2015/06/26/jurgen-habermas-on-faith-and-knowledge/. – May 2, 2018.

In: Religion and Public Life
Editor: David Muskhelishvili

ISBN: 978-1-53618-904-9
© 2021 Nova Science Publishers, Inc.

Chapter 4

SCIENCE AND THE MEDIEVAL CHRISTIAN CHURCH OF THE WEST

Teimuraz Buadze[*]
Faculty of Humanities and Social Studies, Tbilisi, Georgia

ABSTRACT

After the famous books of John William Draper and Andrew Dixon White (John William Draper, *A History of the Conflict between Religion and Science,* (1874), Andrew Dickson White, *A History of the Warfare of Science with Theology in Christendom,* (1896)), many researchers or people with scientist views think that during the Middle Ages the Catholic Church hindered the development of science. This view is directly contradicted by the historical fact that the first universities, by the modern understanding of this word, had been originated in medieval Christian Europe and a modern scientific paradigm different from natural philosophy began to take shape at the abovementioned time and place.

Christianity is a creationist type of monotheistic religion that teaches that God has created the universe out of nothing (ex nihilo) without coercion. Thus, unlike pantheistic religious-philosophical systems, Christianity argues that God and the universe are distinct from one another and that the processes going on are subjects not to purely

---

[*] Corresponding Author's E-mail: teimuraz.buadze@gmail.com.

theological principles and autonomous spiritual instances (Anism) but to God-created laws.

Unlike Hinduism, Buddhism, Gnosticism and dualistic religions, Christianity teaches that the material world is not an illusion or a manifestation of an evil force, but a divine wisdom that the human mind is capable of perception by making observation on nature. This metaphysical environment led to the fact that modern science, as a socio-cultural phenomenon, was born in Christian Europe and not elsewhere, even though Europeans did not possess many scientific facts about other peoples in the era of the origin of science.

With rare exceptions, the Church saw in scientists and science not opponents of the Christian faith but allies in the fight against the occultism.

Keywords: Religion, science, scientism**,** first and second causality, prefigurative, anagogical, natural philosophy, occultism, creationism, pantheism, Gnosticism

Religion and science are the most important factors defining our public life, culture, and civilization. There was a diverse range of different views of God during various epochs, in civilizations and cultures at a place where a line between the religious and the secular must pass, regarding useful methods in gaining scientific knowledge and stemming from the aforementioned, regarding the forms of the existing or possible, desired or impermissible mutual influences between religion and science. Despite this diversity it seems that it will be enough if Christianity is implied in the word "religion" and the natural sciences in "science" for an essential examination of the issue of the interrelationships between religion and science. Because the word "science" - in the modern interpretation of this word - took shape during the 16th-17th centuries in Christian Europe and those who supported the thesis of the seemingly "quarrelsome interrelationship" between religion and science, as a rule, implied the natural sciences more so in the word "science" than the humanitarian ones.

In the opinion of those supporting this thesis, the development of science was hindered most of all in medieval Europe. Since the Christian Church held a dominant position during this period, it was concluded that the main reason for this setback was faith. It is argued that science was conceived in ancient Greece and freely developed there. For an entire millennium beginning from the 5th century, nothing significant had occurred in science due to the negative influence of the Church and a rebirth only began after the Church's influence began to wane around the 16th century (1. Brooke, *Science and Religion*, 33−51.). These people consider the authority of Holy Scripture and the dogmas of the Christian faith as the main factors hindering science. Their views cannot stand up to criticism from a historical, factual, and conceptual standpoint. Because the authority of Holy Scripture and the dogmas are the most essential part of this issue, they must be examined first and then the other things will be dealt with.

It is not possible for the Bible to be considered a book that provides scientific knowledge regarding the world. Only this or that science can provide this knowledge. Science teaches how the universe is organized and the Holy Scriptures however teach how our dependence on the universe must be. According to a famous phrase from centuries ago, "Science tells us how the sky is arranged, the Scriptures however show the way to heaven." (2. Кураев, *Неамериканский миссионер*, 52) If a specific example is cited to illustrate this idea, it is possible to use a train schedule for this purpose. However thoroughly we might study this schedule, it cannot indicate in and of itself as to where exactly we must travel. The direction of travel, the destination are determined by our will, the schedule however expresses an order independent of us. As an analogy to this, the Scriptures speak of the Divine will that our will must be aligned with, science however tries to discover the dominant order in the universe. Because of this, the Scriptures and science do not oppose each other, but instead complement each other. An expression of this is the concept of the "one truth" and "two books" seen with Saint Augustine (3. Lindberg and Numbers, *God and Nature*, 19−48). In accordance with the first one, it is not possible for the truth revealed by the Scriptures to be in opposition to the truth that science and philosophy search for. It is the obligation of a rational mind illuminated by faith to confirm the agreement between them. This goal can always be achieved because there can only be one truth.

According to the second concept, the God who created the universe reveals himself to a person via two supplementary ways. These are the Holy Scriptures revealing Christ's will and laws to us and "the book of the universe" that helps one to see the wisdom of the Creator manifested in the scientific discoveries of laws created by Him. The free Divine will and ordinance active in the universe do not imply an annulment of the God-created laws extant in the universe. The principle of moderate naturalism widespread during the Middle Ages is precisely an expression of this thought based on the principle of the so-called "first and second causality" (4. Thomas Aquinas, *Commentary on Aristotle's Physics*, 129). According to this teaching, God is the primary cause of the universe and he fulfills his will, his acts in this universe through the means of the laws established by Him. This means that everything occurring in the universe can simultaneously be classified on one hand, as an expression of God's will or allowance, or on the second hand, as a result of the laws extant in the universe. Stemming from this, the Church did not see an adversary of the Holy Scriptures in science, but instead it was deeply convinced in the possibility of their agreement. From the very beginning, authoritative theologians considered that it was always possible to interpret the Holy Scriptures and formulate scientific facts in such a way that revelatory truth and science would never oppose each other. Texts of the Holy Scriptures consist mostly of three types of passages carrying moral, prefigurative, and anagogical thoughts. The first type of passage shows the way to moral perfection, with the second type depicting such stories of Biblical characters (Joshua, Isaac, Joseph, et al.) embodying beforehand the coming Messiah and the third kind revealing the mysteries of heaven. In regard to an instrumentalist understanding of science, according to this concept, the primary function of science is to explain scientific facts, turn them into effective instruments from a pragmatic standpoint, and not possess the absolute truth (5. Lindberg and Numbers, *God and Nature,* 76–113). In accordance with this concept, however precisely established scientific facts must be, not one scientific theory can have the pretense of being absolute truth. The facts remain, but theories are constantly changing, with one becoming outdated and another taking its place. Because of this, a theologian is not forced to agree with or categorically deny any particular scientific theory when expounding upon the Holy Scriptures. Since every specific scientific theory offers only a more or less approximate model of reality, with not one of them possibly having the pretense of having the absolute truth, it is impossible for someone to corroborate that science is generally in opposition to revelatory truth even in the case when a certain scientific theory is not in complete agreement with a specific interpretation of a certain place in the Holy Scriptures.

The view according to which science had come into being in the ancient world, freely developed there, with its progress was later being hindered by the Church over the course of a millennium is also incorrect. In reality, the ancient world, whether this be ancient Greece, Egypt, India, or China, does not know science in the modern sense of this word, despite them being able to discover many scientific facts during that epoch (the only exception being mathematics, because it is founded on logic, not experimentation). There was only natural philosophy in the ancient world. Its essence is indicated by this word itself, with it signifying the observation of nature and the underlying philosophy. Natural philosophy is not based on scientific experimentation, but on philosophical speculation, the syllogistic logic of Aristotle, whose fundamental premises or postulates are of a theological nature. For example, astronomy was a part of theology in the ancient world. Despite the rich astronomical knowledge during that epoch and that they were well able to use it for practical purposes, astronomy was still unable to take shape as a science. This was hindered by worldview factors. At that time, even Aristotle and Ptolemy believed that the heavenly bodies were divinities and their movement was not dictated by objective, physical laws, but instead by the will of the gods and theological principles. It was these views themselves that became the foundation for astrological superstitions. Clearly, it was impossible for astronomy to take shape as a science in the modern sense of this word. Christianity brought the teaching that everything in this universe is created, with the sun, moon, planets, and stars seen on Earth being no different from other objects, and that the physical laws established by God are in force everywhere. These views provided the means for Copernicus, Galileo, Newton, and others to turn astronomy into a science.

The nature philosophical principles of Aristotle's "physics" were dominant among Islamic philosophers and scientists during the Hellenic epoch and the Middle Ages as well. Due to Aristotle's immense authority, it was precisely his mistakes that dealt a blow to the development of science. For example, he postulated only on the basis of philosophical speculations that heavy objects fall more quickly to Earth than light ones, that there was no vacuum because "nature is scared of emptiness", and that objects only move when there is an outer force operating on them, etc. In the 13th century, the western Church officially condemned certain principles of Aristotle's metaphysics, greatly weakened the great philosopher's authority, cast doubt on the tenets of his nature philosophy, and stimulated the experimental method of research or modern science (6. Rubenstein, *Aristotle's Children,* 216). Pioneers of modern science required the experimental method in order to rebut the tenets of Aristotelian nature philosophy. The contemporary, modern natural sciences are founded on experiments and mathematical models. In Christian Europe, scientific experiments as well as mathematics began to be used in order to study nature (Plato categorically denied the use of mathematics in order to study earthly phenomena. In his opinion, the usefulness of a mathematical language was only appropriate when speaking of the heavenly bodies and the ideal universe). The Church was not in enmity with the new science, instead it helped develop it because it saw an ally within it to fight against the occultism, magic, astronomy, and alchemy left over from the ancient world. The study of natural philosophical and scientific texts was a required component of theological education at the university level during the Middle Ages (7. Grendler, P. *The universities of the Renaissance,* 2-8). This was the cause of a large portion of scholars being clergy members. For example, Roger Bacon and Copernicus were clergy members. Galileo and Kepler dreamed about being members of the clergy, but they were hindered by certain life circumstances. The philosophical and methodological foundations of modern science attained a full form in the 16th century. This was not by chance because at this time, the Church was wholeheartedly warring against the paganism and occultism brought to life by the Renaissance. This was the period when the counter-reform of the Catholic Church was in opposition to the Protestantism of Luther, thus kindling interest and critical thinking regarding religious issues. It is for this reason that the idea of the birth of science seemingly being a direct result of the diminution of faith is an erroneous opinion.

Now, when modern science has taken on an established, traditional form, it can develop anywhere, but the environment of a particular worldview was necessary during its origins. It was necessary for the views and institutions dominant during that era to be sanctioned for its development. Science can only become a part of culture, a strong social force when scientific research is not perceived as a dissident action. Such an environment was brought by the teaching of Christian creationism, according to which the universe was created out of nothing by one, personal God of his own free will out of love. This teaching implies in itself that the universe is real, it is different from its creator and is governed by objective laws. Since the Creator is a single, loving God, the universe is not dependent on the capricious whims of various divinities, but instead is subordinate to universal, unchangeable, and rational laws. Additionally, human beings have been bestowed with such abilities that enable them to discover these laws (in contrast to Christians, Buddhists and Hindus consider the world to be an illusion; for the Gnostics, the material world is an embodiment of evil. In this context, it is very difficult, even impossible to come up with a concept of objective, unchangeable, scientific laws. Since pantheists equate the universe and its creator to each other, scientific experiments in traditional, pantheistic cultures are perceived more as sacrilege than as research methodology. Non-Christian mysticism (shamanism, the Kabbalah, etc.) teaches that there is an independent spirit or angel behind every object or being governing their fate. Clearly, such traditions are not advantageous to the birth of science, because physics, zoology, biology, etc, turn out to be offshoots of angelology or demonology). Since the universe was created by an omnipotent God, it could have been different, in principle. This means that the study of the universe is only possible by observing it, experimenting with it and not by only making logical conclusions from the loftiest metaphysical principles, like natural philosophy does. It is precisely due to the aforementioned facts that modern science came into being only in Christian Europe and not anywhere else, despite Christian Europe at that time almost not standing out from other civilized peoples in view of the knowledge of scientific facts.

At the conclusion of the paper, it must be noted that the opposition of religion and science is not desirable for either of them. If a believer is in opposition to scientific knowledge, he is acting like a fanatic, an obscurantist. On the other hand, without the moral values inspired by religion, technology can become a supremely dangerous force for us, with the history of the use of the atomic bomb being an example.

REFERENCES

Brooke, John Hedley. *Science and Religion: Some Historical Perspectives*. Cambridge: Cambridge University Press, 1991.

Кураев Андрей, *Неамериканский миссионер/Материалы к реферату на тему "Религия и наука"*, Москва, 2010. [*Non-American missionary / Materials for the essay on the topic "Religion and Science"*]

Grendler, P. F. "The universities of the Renaissance and Reformation". *Renaissance Quarterly*, 57, 2004.

Lindberg, David C., and Ronald L. Numbers, eds. *God and Nature: Historical Essays on the Encounter between Christianity and Science*. Berkeley, CA: University of California Press, 1986.

Rubenstein, Richard E. *Aristotle's Children: How Christians, Muslims, and Jews Rediscovered Ancient Wisdom and Illuminated the Middle Ages*. Houghton Mifflin Harcourt, 2004.

Thomas Aquinas, *Commentary on Aristotle's Physics*, trans. Richard J. Blackwell, Richard J. Spath & W. Edmund Thirlkel, Yale U.P., 1963.

In: Religion and Public Life
Editor: David Muskhelishvili
ISBN: 978-1-53618-904-9
© 2021 Nova Science Publishers, Inc.

Chapter 5

THE KEY PRESUPPOSITION OF LIBERAL THEOLOGY

Daniel von Wachter[*]
Professor of Philosophy, International Academy of Philosophy
in the Principality of Liechtenstein

ABSTRACT

A central claim of liberal theology is that miracles are incompatible with science. The most plausible version of this claim states that miracles are violations of the laws of nature. This paper argues that this is not true because the laws of nature describe not actual events and regularities of succession but forces. There is nothing in science that is incompatible with, or evidence against, the existence of miracles.

Keywords: liberal theology, miracles, laws of nature

---

[*] Corresponding Author's E-mail: epost@von-wachter.de.

LIBERAL THEOLOGY

In this chapter I want to draw your attention to an idea about the relationship between religion and science which was a central cause of what is called "liberal theology" in the West. By this term I mean the movement in theology that is represented by Friedrich Schleiermacher (1768–1834), Ernst Troeltsch (1865–1923), and Rudolf Bultmann (1884–1976). They called themselves "Christian theologians" although they rejected many doctrines that hitherto generally were considered to be essential to Christianity. In particular, liberal theologians claim that we "cannot" believe in miracles or, more generally, in divine interventions any more.

The doctrines about God and salvation which traditional Christian theology considered essential to Christian faith are rejected in liberal theology. The change from traditional Christian theology to this liberal theology is therefore very big. A liberal theologian might claim that he discovered the true essence of the Christian doctrines and therefore changed their interpretation, but whatever view you take on this, the change in the beliefs is very big.

Liberal theology has dramatically changed all the mainline Protestant churches, beginning with the German Protestant state churches, and later also the Roman Catholic Church. That is, in these churches forms of liberal theology have been accepted by many or by the majority of theology professors and ministers. It is no exaggeration that without liberal theology, the religion and thinking of large segments of the population could well have developed very differently. And therefore history could well have developed very differently.

FRIEDRICH SCHLEIERMACHER, THE CHURCH FATHER OF THE 19TH CENTURY

Friedrich Schleiermacher is sometimes called the "Church father" of the 19th century. And rightly so, because, while there had been others before him who rejected traditional Christian doctrine in similar ways, Schleiermacher brought liberal theology into the faculties of theology of German universities and into the German state churches.

On the 21st of January, 1787, Schleiermacher, while he was a student of an evangelical seminary, wrote to his father that he cannot believe any more that Jesus was the "eternal, true God" and that "his death was a substitutionary atonement". In later writings he is more articulate about his reasons for rejecting traditional Christian doctrine. His main reason is that belief in miracles is incompatible with science.

> If you consider the contemporary state of the natural sciences, what do you expect [...] for our Protestant Christianity? Me thinks that we will have to learn to do without what many are still accustomed to regard as inseparably bound to the essence of Christianity. [...] The concept of a miracle will not be able to exist in its present form.

If the Church, Schleiermacher thinks, continues to teach that there were divine interventions in the universe, then it will contradict science and hence its doctrine will become untenable, the Church will become irrelevant, and theology can no longer have a place in the university. So Schleiermacher's main reason for rejecting Christian doctrine and forming liberal theology is his claim that belief in miracles is incompatible with science. Troeltsch, Bultmann, and many others have similar reasons. They say that one "cannot" believe in miracles any more.

As Schleiermacher did not simply want to say that Christian doctrine is false and that Christianity should therefore be given up, he changed the meanings of the traditional Christian doctrinal statements. He attributed new meanings to them, which do not contain anything anymore that Schleiermacher did not believe. In particular, they do not contain any claims of divine interventions.

MIRACLES AND DIVINE INTERVENTIONS

I shall now argue that there is no rational reason for the claim that divine interventions are impossible or incompatible with science. For this, first we need to understand what a divine intervention is, and for this we first need an idea of what a causal process is, because divine interventions are interventions *in* causal processes. Examples of causal processes are a rolling billiard ball and a tidal wave. Causal processes have a direction, they are heading in a certain direction. The billiard ball at time t_1 is heading towards falling into the pocket at time t_2. At time t_1 the billiard ball is in a way programmed so that it will be at certain positions at certain later times if nothing stops it. In Chile on February 27, 2010 at 6:39 UTC, five minutes after the earthquake, there was a tidal wave heading towards reaching Easter Island at 12:05 UTC. Also a thing's persisting in time is a causal process. The billiard ball's existence and being as it is at t_1 is a cause of its existence at t_2. Things are, or are constituted by, causal processes.

A divine intervention is an event brought about by God directly which occurs instead of an event which a causal process would have brought about if God had not intervened. It is thus an event which God brings about and which stops some causal process. More precisely:

> A divine intervention is an event which is brought about by God directly and which is incompatible with an event towards which a causal process was heading.

If God lets Peter walk on water, he brings about his position above the water so that he stays above the water instead of sinking into the water, which is what the causal processes, driven by gravitational force, would lead to. If God raises Jesus from the dead, he makes his body alive when the causal processes were directed towards the body staying dead and decaying.

Miracles are a kind of divine intervention. They are divine interventions through which God shows something to somebody. A different kind of divine intervention would be God creating a certain animal, for example, so that the existence of that animal is not just the result of causal processes. Schleiermacher and other liberal theologians took miracles to be impossible or incompatible with science because they are divine interventions. So are divine interventions compatible with science?

MIRACLES AS "VIOLATIONS OF THE LAWS OF NATURE"

The most promising way to defend the incompatibility of miracles and science is to say that the laws of nature exclude the existence of divine interventions. Thus David Hume said that miracles would be *"violations of the laws of nature"*. If this were true, that would be a powerful argument against miracles, because all the evidence that supports the laws of nature that we know of today – the experiments and the observations – would at the same time be evidence against the existence of miracles. That evidence would show that there are no miracles without us having to examine the evidence for the alleged miracles. For example, we then would not have to examine how credible the reports of the disciples to have seen the risen Jesus are, how credible the reports about what the disciples said are, etc. We would have a simple, quick, and powerful argument against *all* miracles. Hume himself took his argument to be such an argument:

> A miracle is a violation of the laws of nature; and as a firm and unalterable experience has established these laws, the proof against a miracle, from the very nature of the fact, is as entire as any argument from experience can possibly be imagined. (*Enquiry*, § 90)

This is based on the assumption that laws of nature entail *regularities of succession* of the form:

> Every event of type *x* is followed by an event of type *y*.

In addition Hume assumes that (always or necessarily)

> Equal events are followed by equal events.

Every event is therefore an element of a regularity of succession, and every event is governed by laws of nature. Remember, a divine intervention is an event brought about by God directly which occurs instead of an event which a causal process would have brought about had God not intervened. This entails that a divine intervention is an event of type z that follows an event of type x, where events of type x on other occasions are followed by events of type y. So, given the aforementioned assumptions, a divine intervention is a violation of the laws of nature. It is an event about which the laws of nature say that it does not occur.

WHAT DO THE LAWS OF NATURE SAY?

Let us examine the claim that miracles would be violations of the laws of nature. What do the laws say? What, for example, does the law of gravitation, $F = m_1 m_2/d^2$, say?

The letter F on the left side of the equation signifies a Newtonian force. On the right side of the equation there are the masses of the bodies, their distance, and the gravitational constant. The law says that for every two bodies there is a certain force pulling to them towards each other. Simply put, the law of gravitation says that every two bodies attract each other to a certain degree, depending on their masses, their distance, and the gravitational constant. More generally, laws are statements of the following form:

> In situations of kind x there are forces of kind y.

So does a divine intervention violate such laws? Does it violate what the laws say? The laws say that there are forces of certain kinds in situations of certain kinds. A divine intervention violates that if and only if it abolishes a force. Does it? No. If God makes Peter walk on water, the gravitational force pulling him down is still there. God just counteracts that force by making Peter be above the water. Therefore divine interventions are not violations of the laws of nature.

In order to intervene, God does not need to abolish any forces because forces can be counteracted. That is evident also from the fact that forces can be superimposed. If there is a force F acting on a body, it accelerates the body with $a = F/m$ only if nothing else is acting on the body. It does not accelerate thus if, for example, another force, an animal, a man, a ghost, or God is acting on the body.

John Stuart Mill therefore wrote:

> All laws of causation, in consequence of their liability to be counteracted, require to be stated in words affirmative of tendencies only, and not of actual results.

By saying that laws require to be stated in words not affirmative "of actual results", Mill means that laws of nature do not say that all events of type x are always followed by events of type y. That is, laws do not entail regularities of succession. The belief in regularities of succession is not supported by laws and observation, it was invented by philosophers without basis in experience. There are no regularities of succession because if at one occasion an event of type x causes an event of type y, at another occasion where there is an event of type x, there may be something which prevents it from causing an event of type y. What laws do entail are conditional predictions of the following form:

> If a situation is of kind x and nothing else is affecting what will follow, then an event of type y will follow.

That forces can be counteracted reflects something that we know from our ordinary experience of material things. Deterministic philosophers like Thomas Hobbes and Immanuel Kant taught that physical causal processes are unstoppable. Hobbes claimed: "Every event is necessitated by things antecedent." Kant stated in his principle of causality: "Every event is determined by a cause according to constant laws." That is false because every causal process can be stopped. It cannot stop by accident, but it can be stopped by something that acts causally upon it. A physical process can be stopped by another physical process, by an animal, or by a human being. And therefore it can also be stopped by God.

Determinists would reply that if a process is stopped by another physical process, that intersection of processes was determined too. It is true that that intersection was also governed by laws of nature. The two processes that run into each other constitute one bigger process governed by the laws of nature. But still, the possibility of one process being stopped by another shows that physical processes can be stopped. A process stops if there is something that stops it. Bigger processes are not more necessary and unstoppable than smaller processes, they just require more powerful things to stop them.

In summary, divine interventions do not violate the laws of nature, because the laws of nature say only what forces there are in which kind of situation. Forces can be counteracted. Forces can be counteracted by other physical forces, by animals, or by human beings. And of course they can also be counteracted also by God. The laws say what forces there are. In a miracle, God does not annihilate any forces, he just counteracts them. Therefore miracles are not violations of the laws of nature.

The question of whether there are divine interventions cannot be answered by just referring to the laws of nature or to some metaphysical principle. It can only be answered by examining the evidence for particular divine interventions.

Liberal theologians say that we have to revise Christian doctrine because science excludes belief in divine interventions. But science and rationality do no such thing. Divine interventions are perfectly compatible with the laws of nature and with science. Hence there is no reason here for abandoning biblical and traditional Christian doctrine.

REFERENCES

Lülmann, C. (1907). *Schleiermacher, Der Kirchenvater des 19. Jahrhunderts*. Tübingen: Mohr. [*Schleiermacher, the church father of the 19th century*.]

Mill, John Stuart. (1843). *A System of Logic Ratiocinative and Inductive*. New York: Harper, 1882. http://gutenberg.org/etext/27942.

Schleiermacher, Friedrich. (1829). 'Sendschreiben an Lücke'. *Theologische Studien und Kritiken*, 2, 254–284, 481–532. ['Letter to gap'. *Theological studies and reviews*]

———. (1860). *Aus Schleiermacher's Leben, Erster Band*. Berlin: Georg Reimer. [*From Schleiermacher's Life, Volume One*]

Wachter, Daniel von. (2015). 'Miracles Are Not Violations of the Laws of Nature Because Laws Do Not Entail Regularities'. *European Journal for Philosophy of Religion*, 7 (4), 37–60.

In: Religion and Public Life
Editor: David Muskhelishvili
ISBN: 978-1-53618-904-9
© 2021 Nova Science Publishers, Inc.

Chapter 6

THE COEXISTENCE MODEL OF RELIGIOUS AND SECULAR DISCOURSES: SAINT ANTHIM THE IBERIAN

Anastasia Zakariadze[*]

Member of the Representative Council of Ivane Javakhishvili Tbilisi State University, Head of Anthim the Iberian Scientific Research Center for Philosophy and Theology, Tbilisi, Georgia

ABSTRACT

In the age of reason and knowledge St. Anthim aimed to base a new paradigm of Western Enlightenment on the teachings of the Apostolic Fathers. He entered a new field of discourse so that his communicative texts would be understandable and admissible to the epoch, relating a new system of values to a new sanctified style of life.

Keywords: Saint Anthim the Iberian, enlightenment, rationalism, religious and secular discourses, social doctrine

---

[*] Corresponding Author's E-mail: anastasia.zakariadze@tsu.ge.

The task of bringing modernity out of the spiritual crisis and saving the Western Church comes to the fore of modern western theologians. There is a question, how did it happen that spiritual and cultural manifestations of rationality, modernization, and legitimacy gain universal significance in the West? The philosopher and sociologist Max Weber has written a special work regarding the sociology of religion *The Protestant Ethic and the Spirit of Capitalism*, in which he tries to prove that the merit of Protestant ethics is the establishment of a new system of values - a new sanctioned lifestyle, a new type of behavior (Weber, 2005: 216). An individual should be focused on purposeful labour, thrift, calculation, self-control, personal dignity based on self-knowledge, the strict observance of obligations and responsibilities. The "inner asceticism" practiced by Protestants was presented as the main lever for the bringing up a new man, for the establishment of new values. Religious discourse will not be able to go the way of rationalization and modernization without it. The obvious example of the process of secularization of religious discourse is observed in the early American Enlightenment, namely in the Enlightenment scheme of Benjamin Franklin. The main actor in this model is a man who purposefully strives for happiness as a supreme good. This model is based on thirteen moral virtues which a man must follow in order to achieve his goal - a "happy end". These virtues are temperance, silence, order, resolution, frugality, industry, sincerity, justice, moderation, cleanliness, tranquility, chastity, and humility. Franklin characterizes this last virtue with the following words: "Imitate Jesus and Socrates."[1] This is some kind of a test of perfection. Franklin's project of self-perfection combines the Enlightenment ideal of the pursuit of perfection and the idea of self-criticism characteristic of Puritan philosophy with enviable skill. Franklin teaches us - one should strive for perfection and at the same time should be

---

[1] For more details about these issues, see the studies: Isaacson, Walter (2003), Benjamin Franklin: An American Life. New York: Simon & Schuster; Brands, H. W (2010), The First American: The Life and Times of Benjamin Franklin; Dr. Alan Houston (2008), Benjamin Franklin and the Politics of Improvement, Yale U. P.; J. A. Leo Lemay (2008), The Life of Benjamin Franklin, Volume 3: Soldier, Scientist, and Politician, 1748–1757. U. Pennsylvania Press, and in Franklin's autobiography - Franklin, Benjamin. (2007, fir. ed. 1900,) The Autobiography of Benjamin Franklin: Poor Richard's Almanac and other papers. New York: A. L. Burt Co., p.38.

permanently self-critical. Franklin experienced and traveled this way himself. Franklin's so-called theory of perfection bears the marks of the famous theory of Behaviorism of the 20th century.

Since the epoch of the Enlightenment, such efforts ultimately acquire the image of liberal Christianity due to attempts by Paul Tillich at a revision of Christian Orthodoxy. The orientations of theological theories sharply turn from being metaphysical-philosophical to practical-sociological. These efforts are mainly aimed at adapting theology to the modern socio-cultural situation. Despite the ambitious goal of reflecting an adequate picture of the process of religion and secularization, the efforts of American theologians reach an impasse. Such, are, for example, the efforts of Michael Novak and Harvey Cox to bring Western theology out of the crisis by the help of the pragmatic God of the secular city.[2] In each such theory, a man "thrown" into the universe and left without support depends only on himself.

At the early stage of the development of the Western Enlightenment, Saint Anthimos of Iberia, an Orthodox theologian and philosopher, faced a difficult problem - he had to overcome the difficulties of the Enlightenment, the intellectual trend dominating at that time. The era of the "domination of reason" - rationalism - has become a general cultural phenomenon since the Renaissance. It penetrates science, philosophy, literature, art, everyday life, institutions of public administration, and theology. Specialization and professionalism are the signs of this process.

The requirement of the epoch is the creation of such a social system, which, on the one hand, presupposes rational calculation, the widespread use of technical knowledge and science and, at the same time, the preservation of justice.

---

[2] Novak introduces the term "the spirit of democratic capitalism". He implies the union of three factors within it. They are: a market economy, basic human rights - the right to life, liberty, and the pursuit of happiness - and institutes founded on the ideals of freedom and universal justice. Novak believes that within the framework of this model it is possible to overcome the difficulty that faces religious discourse today. Cox says: "Theological honesty makes us admit that "God died" (Cox: 1966, p. 228). The theological principle of "God exists" has lost its significance, first of all, because of social reasons; its natural environment is rural culture, and it is quite unnecessary in the socio-cultural practice of the modern city. The formation of urban civilization and the weakening of traditional religion are two signs and two interconnected tendencies of our epoch.

Kant's famous expression is that enlightenment is man's emergence from his self-imposed immaturity, and since that moment man should begin to live only based on his own mind. The mind becomes an absolute ruler, for which only circumstances explained by common sense and natural laws are acceptable. The vector of the main blow of the epoch is directed against traditional values, traditional religious hierarchy and canon, and existing forms of public administration. The disintegration of the traditional scheme of values occurs in every sphere: in theology - theism should be substituted by deism and atheism; the substantiation of God must only take place within the framework of reason (Berkley, Kant); in social and political life, the forms of absolute government should be substituted by democratic ones, the official reformation of church administration should take place.

Saint Anthimos's task in the epoch of reason and knowledge is to establish a new paradigm of enlightenment on the grounds of the holy Fathers' teachings. To do this, he has to enter the realm of this new discourse in such a way that his communication would be acceptable and understandable for the epoch. In other words, the traditional system of values should adapt to a new sanctioned lifestyle, and thus make the task accomplished - not an introduction of a new type of behavior, but a "placement" of morality within the framework of classical absolutism.

Greek intellectuals had acknowledged Anthimos of Iberia as a great thinker and theologian already during his lifetime. The assessments of his contemporaries have survived to the present day.[3] For example, Giorgi Mayorta, a famous scribe working at the court of the Prince of Wallachia, St. Constantin Brâncoveanu, said: "God sent us the light from the country of the wise Iberians - Metropolitan Anthimosof Hungary-Wallachia".

---

[3] Studies on the life and work of Anthimos have mainly been conducted in the Romanian-language academic sphere. Of these, we have chosen the studies of Gabriel Stempl, Archimandrite MikhaelStanchiu, Popescu, Bratulescu, and others. The interest in this great figure was mainly of a historiographical character in Georgia. An intensive study and translation of his works, an academic study of his theological ideas, an evaluation of his merits, and the results of studies of modern European scholars in a new way began in 2008 (see: I. Brachuli, A. Zakariadze, V. Ramishvili, A. Kshutashvili, D. Jalaghonia, "Anthimos of Iberia - Georgian-European Dialogue" and a collection in two volumes "Georgia and the European World - A Cultural-Philosophical Dialogue").

The dissemination of knowledge and the education of the parish by different means lies at the heart of the educational paradigm of Anthimos of Iberia. First of all, he uses preaching to achieve this goal. A deep and thorough knowledge of the texts of the New and Old Testaments, the teachings of the Holy Fathers, as well as of modern scientific texts - works in natural sciences, medicine, and philosophy - can be clearly seen from the sermons of St. Anthimos of Iberia. He often cites Aristotle, Plato, the Neoplatonists, as well as philosophers of the Antique and other periods. His knowledge of the history of the Church and the world is also clearly visible. People have studied not only spirituality, but also the natural sciences, philosophy, and even medicine from his sermons.

The second vector of his educational activity involves the opening of a school within a monastery. To this end, Anthimos founded a school. In the 6th chapter of the typikon of the Monastery of Anthimos of Iberia the system according to which the education of children should be conducted is clearly indicated. Teaching poor children is considered preferable. "Three poor children who want study, have to be given six Ban each annually, as well as a chokha for two zloty, a shirt, a pair of shoes for Easter; the age of these three children should not be less than 10 years or exceed 15 years. This charity has to be provided to them for four years, as during this period a child could be able to master the Slavic and Greek languages, and then others would be accepted on their places. If any of them wants to become a monk and stay in the monastery, let him be accepted! The monastery should give them textbooks. After graduation, the abbot should hand each of them a letter: if any of them are going to get married, he would be able to come and get 15 thalers as a help for wedding" (Anthimos of Iberia, Didaches, 2016: 203).

It is interesting that according to the will of Anthimos of Iberia, the monastery was obliged to give a dowry to graduates of the seminary if they were married, and if any of them was consecrated as a priest, the monastery had to give him the full vestments of a priest, a chalice and dish and, in general, everything necessary for church services, and "if someone wants to become a priest, he must be given 13 additional thalers; 8 thalers from this sum is for his consecration as a deacon and a priest, and he can keep for himself the remaining 5 thalers for serving a funeral" (Anthimos of Iberia, Didaches, 2016: 204).

St. Antimos obliged educated married priests to teach children the subjects and church rules as defined by the teaching plan; and children were charged to come to the church at dawn, during vespers, and for church services; "and if someone wants to become a priest, he must also be taught the church service rules" (Anthimos of Iberia, Didaches, 2016: 204).

St. Anthimos of Iberia paid special attention to the education of priests. Separate chapters are dedicated to these issues in his *Typikon and Laws*. He substantially proves that the origin of all evil is ignorance.

"As there are many uneducated priests among you, you do not know how to compose them and neither common Christians know how to teach you to write them. That is why there are so many quarrels, trials, lawsuits, making oaths, the writing of letters of damnation, and other evils. That's why we define the rule of composing wills, which must be fulfilled" (Anthimos of Iberia, Didaches, 2016: 251).

Anthimos of Iberia founded the first public library in Romania at the Monastery of All Saints built by him. Most of the copies in the book fund are his personal contribution. He devotes a separate chapter to the problem of preserving the library fund in his "Typicon".

The main vector of Anthimos' social education project of is publishing - the main innovation of the Enlightenment. Most of the books were translated and published by his means at the printing houses of Bucharest, Snagov, Rymnik, and Targovishte. During his 26 years of activity in Wallachia, Anthimos published 64 books: he was the author of 4 of them, wrote introductions for 10 of them, provided notes and commentary for 6 books, wrote verses for 5 books, and translated 6 books from Greek, Arabic, and Old Slavic into Romanian. In this respect, the merit of Anthimos of Iberia before his motherland is of particular importance. It is well known that in 1708 he sent one of his best disciples, Mikhai Ishtvanovich, to Georgia along with all the equipment of a Georgian-language printing house, previously printed antimenses, and matrices of various icons and ornaments. Since 1709, Mikhai Ishtvanovich had printed many ecclesiastical books in Tbilisi: the Gospels, Psalms, prayers, the

Book of hours, kontakions. In other words, St. Anthimos of Iberia took care so that the Georgian people would have had more spiritual nourishment, and considered books, prayers especially, as the most important sources for it. That is why the books printed first in the printing press sent by Anthimos were the Gospel, Acts, and other ecclesiastic books. Beside the books, antimenses were also printed in the printing house of Anthimos of Iberia.[4]

Each year, the monastery was obliged to take care of some poor young men and girls of marriageable age. The monastery had to completely pay their dowry in the form of clothes and a certain amount of money. Particular attention was paid to helping the poor - both with money and food. There were detailed rules on how to clothe the naked and how to marry poor girls, and also to help those foreigners who "came to this country because of poverty". The monastery had to give them shelter and feed them. This rule is obligatory for the monastery even today. "We see in the Holy Gospel that Our Lord Jesus Christ does not consider anyone worthy of the kingdom of heaven unless he/she has not done kind deeds in the earthly life: have not helped the poor, have not fed the hungry, have not given to drink, have not clothed the naked, have not comforted strangers, the diseased, and prisoners" (Anthimos of Iberia, Didaches, 2016: 205).

St. Anthimos took care of prisoners. The monastery had to allocate a certain amount of money "for prisoners every Saturday during the whole year, for every fifty two weeks" (Anthimos of Iberia, Didaches, 2016: 205).

It is worth noting that the rule of visiting the sick, as mandatory, was extended to all infirm people - "The abbot, hieromonks, and priests - as soon as they learn about the illness of any person, whether he/she is their relative or stranger, a man or woman, a resident of this or that district -

---

[4] The letter sent to the Patriarch of Jerusalem ChrisantNotara in 1707 is the primary source in which Anthimos writes, that he prepares matrix for printing Georgian-language antimin. Georgian-language antimin, mentioned in the letter, was printing for the Orthodox Church of Georgia. Unfortunately, we could not find this antimin printed by Anthimos. There is an oral tradition, according to which it should be stored in the depositories of the Museum of Art History.

they will have to visit him/her or send some experienced priest who can calm the patient" (Anthimos of Iberia, Didaches, 2016: 205).

At the same time, in his *Chapters of Laws*, St. Anthimos forbids the clergymen to perform any civil activity devoid of common moral norms. "I order you, priests and deacons, do not interfere in civil affairs - in lying, cunning, flattery, making oaths, false promises, and other similar things which cause excitement and suspicion in people; particularly avoid trading, as you will be punished for it" (Anthimos of Iberia, Didaches, 2016: 246), and immediately adds: "None of the priests should dare sell wine from their home or oblige their wives or servants to do so. But if anybody breaks this order and performs this unworthy and wrong deed he will be deprived of the grace of the priesthood and will be enlisted in the ranks of ignorant peasants" (Anthimos of Iberia, Didaches, 2016: 245). The absolute freedom of the monastery from the civil government, its inviolability and full independence are especially emphasized in Anthimos' project. "The monastery should be completely free; It should not obey anyone and nobody should be its master, neither the prince of the country, nor bishop, who will take my place after me, nor other lords" (Anthimos of Iberia, Didaches, 2016: 210).

The advantage of the paradigm worked out by Anthimos is founded on a view based on the teachings of the holy fathers, that the main vectors of man's being are conditioned and determined by Christ. The basis of his thinking is the cognition of God, the cognition of the essence of the world and life, and the main aspiration of his life, his destination is the salvation of the soul.

St. Anthimos tells us about a key idea of his theological and practical activity on the very first page of the introduction of the *Typikon of the Monastery of Anthimos of Iberia*, which summarizes his thoughts and makes them exemplary for overcoming modern challenges. "Kindness is not kindness if it is not done well" (Anthimos of Iberia, Didaches, 2016: 200). Anthimos of Iberia often cites the Holy Scriptures, the Acts of the Apostles, and the works of the holy fathers in his sermons and other works in order to strengthen this position. "Paul knew that kind deeds help a man to save his soul, that is why in the 13th chapter of his Epistle to the

Hebrews he teaches us not to forget and always fulfill his admonitions: "Do not neglect to do good and to share what you have, for such sacrifices are pleasing to God" (Anthimos of Iberia, Didaches, 2016: 200).

The social project of St. Antimos seems to us a successful example of coexistence with secularism in the sphere of Christian discourse.

REFERENCES

Anthimos of Iberia (2016), *Didaches and Other Works,* Tbilisi, Dobera.

Brachuli I., Zakariadze, A. Ramishvili, V. Cshutashvili, A.D. Jalagonia (2016). *Anthimos of Iberia - Georgian-European Dialogue,* Tbilisi, Dobera.

Brands, H.W (2010), *The First American: The Life and Times of Benjamin Franklin.*

Brătulescu, Victor, (1956), *Antim Ivireanul miniaturist și sculptor,* în rev. Biserica Ortodoxă Română, LXXIV nr. 8-9, p. 766-774. [*Anthim The Iberian miniaturist and sculptor,* in rev. Romanian Orxodox Church.]

Cox, Harvey Gallagher & Callahan, Daniel (1966), *The Secular City Debate,* New York: Macmillan.

Cox, Harvey Gallagher (1965), *The Secular City: Secularization and Urbanization in Theological Perspective;* Collier Books, 25th anniversary edition 1990.

Franklin, Benjamin (2007, fir.ed.1900), *The Autobiography of Benjamin Franklin: Poor Richard's Almanac and other papers.* New York: A.L. Burt Co.

Georgia and the European World - *A Cultural-Philosophical Dialogue,* Vol.1 (2008), Tbilisi, publishing house T.S.U.

Georgia and the European World - *A Cultural-Philosophical Dialogue,* Vol.1 (2008), Tbilisi, publishing house T.S.U.

Houston, Alan (2008), *Benjamin Franklin and the Politics of Improvement.* Yale U.P. J. A.

Isaacson, Walter (2003), *Benjamin Franklin: An American Life.* New York: Simon & Schuster.

Lemay, Leo (2008), *The Life of Benjamin Franklin,* Volume 3: Soldier, Scientist, and Politician, 1748–1757. U. of Pennsylvania Press.

Novak, Michael (1982), *The Spirit of Democratic Capitalism.* Harvard.

Pinckaers, Servais (1995), *The Sources of Christian Ethics.* Washington, D.C.: Catholic University of America Press.

Popescu, Teodor (1956), Antim Ivireanul, apostolşimucenic al drepteicredinţe, în "*Biserica Ortodoxă Română*", LXXIV p. 853-863. [Antim Ivireanul, apostle and martyr of the true faith, in the *"Romanian Orthodox Church"*]

Preot Niculae Şerbănescu (1956), *Antim Ivireanul tipograf,* în rev: "B.O.R."[*Anthim the Iberian typograph*, in rev: "B.O.R."] nr. 8-9/1956. p.690-760.

Ştrempel, Gabriel (1997), *Antim Ivireanul.* Bucureşti: Editura Academiei Române.

In: Religion and Public Life
Editor: David Muskhelishvili
ISBN: 978-1-53618-904-9
© 2021 Nova Science Publishers, Inc.

Chapter 7

THE PROBLEM OF THE COMPATIBILITY OF THEOLOGICAL AND CIVIL SUBJECTS IN GREEK AND ALEXANDRIAN CHRISTIAN SCHOOLS

Avtandil Asatiani[*]
Georgian Technical University, Tbilisi, Georgia

ABSTRACT

The school of Alexandria preferred Plato's methodology. The main problem for Alexandrian theology was the relationship between man and deity, which provided a rational basis for belief, while the method of teaching was considered to be an allegorical explanation of the Bible.

The compatibility of theological and secular subjects in the Greco-Alexandrian Christian school is clearly evidenced by the work and views of Pantene, Clement of Alexandria and Origen, indicating a pluralistic direction of the Alexandrian Christian school.

The pre-Christian school of Alexandria not only allowed the teaching of the seven free arts (trivium-quadrium), but also recognized their propaedeutic significance and full compatibility with the teaching of theological subjects.

---

[*] Corresponding Author's E-mail: avtandil110@gmail.com.

Keywords: Greco-Alexandrian Christian School, compatibility of religious and secular subjects.

Pagan-Hellenic, Judaic and Christian schools occupy a special place in the educational history of Alexandria. The Hellenic school was the oldest, and is connected with Mouseion. The Judaic school was ancient as well, and the Christian school appeared when the Greek and Judaic schools were engulfed by a crisis of ideas. Yet many scholars do not share such a generalization and cast doubt on the very existence of the Christian school (Losev, 1960: 127).

Researcher G. Simone characterizes the pagan schools of Alexandria during Ptolemy's epoch as the first eclectic, mystic, and pantheistic schools (Asatiani, 2007: 29).

Aristobulus and Philo are representatives of the Judaic-Alexandrian religious school. It is Philo of Alexandria who is considered to be the one determining the direction of the Judeo-Alexandrian school. He is closest to the Christian school of Alexandria. His ideas are the transitional stage from Judaism to Christianity.

The researcher Gieseler (Gieseler, 1831: 86) confirms the influence of the Jewish tradition on Christian scholars. He was the person who singled out the two essential features of Alexandrian theology shared by both Christians and Jews: the rejection of anthropomorphism in the teaching about God and the assertion of personal freedom in the teaching about man.

Alexandria became a place of rapprochement for Eastern and Western worldviews. As the researcher Vachero remarks, the aim of Alexandrism was not only the reconciliation of the religious and philosophical, but also the unity of Eastern and Western in every sphere of a worldview. Christianity faced the necessity to master all the achievements of Greek civilization "in order to not disappear from the East" (Vachero, 1846: 51). So, Christian philosophers have inherited the Judeo-Alexandrian way of thinking as a synthesis of Eastern and Western elements, and not only as an experience of biblical apologetics.

But the incarnated and resurrected Savior was the most solid foundation strengthening the Christian teaching in opposing pagan philosophy and Judaism. And it precisely determined that "scholars who led the Alexandrian Christian school began to affirm the divinity and truth of the religion" (Prat, 1843: 76).

The religious educational ideas of early Christian pedagogy were disseminated in the antique world as a counterbalance to the state educational system of Rome, and during the first stage, it developed within the framework of Judaic pedagogy. It should be also taken into account that the rich traditions of Hellenistic education preceded the Christian school of Alexandria (supposedly founded in 179), which had been retained there for a rather long period. As the history of Eusebius confirms, the teaching of free subjects started here very early (at the beginning of the 2nd century) together with Christian teaching, which means that scholars of that time had tried to achieve the harmonious synthesis of knowledge and faith.

Both the philosophers of the Antique epoch (Socrates, Plato) and the fathers of the Christian church paid particular attention to the comprehension of truth through education. It is clear that the connection between early Christianity and Judaic pedagogy is unquestionable since there is an obvious compatibility of the priorities between them mainly manifested in the recognition of a teacher's status, the religious direction of bringing up children, and the irrational understanding of human consciousness.

Christianity and Antiquity have some common points of intersection and ideals, but the difference between them is much greater. Christianity has developed completely different views about children. Children were considered imperfect creatures in Antique pedagogy, and Christianity, on the contrary, categorically rejected the criminal infanticide used in relation to helpless children. If the Sophists declared the man of the Antique epoch as "the measure of all things", Christianity recognized God as the creator of the universe. According to the Christian tradition, an ideal upbringing is not only acquiring knowledge but being in the image and likeness of God, i.e., living according to the divine will. In the New Testament the idea that "the body is the enemy of soul" is rejected in contrast to the Pythagorean doctrine on the confrontation of the body and soul. Paul the Apostle expressed a different idea about it: "Do you not know that your bodies are temples of the Holy Spirit, who is in you" (1 Corinthians 6: 19). So, if Antique thought put the earthly existence of man in the centre of the universe, Christianity, on the contrary, recognized the primacy of eternal human values. The fathers of the Christian Church contraposed the salvation of the soul, mutual assistance, forgiveness, love, obedience, asceticism and other Christian virtues to such ideals of the Hellenistic world as the cult of education, philosophy, a beautiful and healthy body, and self-affirmation.

The superiority of faith over knowledge came to the fore in Christian education. Besides, particular attention was paid to the connection of teaching with a religious, moral upbringing and the importance of instilling diligence was well understood. The words of the Apostle Paul confirm precisely this: "The one who is unwilling to work shall not eat" (II Thessalonians 3:10)

The commandments of the Old Testament - "Thou shalt not kill", "Thou shalt not steal", "Thou shalt love thy neighbour" and others -which were not only ethical principles in biblical Judaism, but also legal norms, are explained in the Gospel in a new way. That is why the pedagogy of the Old Testament is the pedagogy of law, that is, of religion. In contrast to it, the pedagogy of the New Testament, i.e., Christian pedagogy, is the pedagogy of faith and love.

During the crisis of Antique pedagogy, Christianity truly found itself before the dilemma of defining the essence of education. Some cardinal pedagogical problems had to be solved: 1. Was it necessary for Christians to study the seven free arts (trivium-quadrivium) established in classical Greek-Roman education?

2. Was it possible to combine the Holy Scripture with these sciences? It was the answer to these questions that became the main problem for early Christian didactics: some clearly negative, compromised, and unequivocally positive opinions were expressed. The views of Philo of Alexandria (28-21 BC - 41-49 AD), a philosopher from this epoch,

confirm exactly this. He likes those works that contribute to the ideological transition from Judaism to Christianity.

Plato's methodology was dominant in the Alexandrian school. The main problems of Alexandrian theology were the relationship between man and Godimplying a rational basis for faith, and a method of teaching explaining the Bible in allegorical terms. The compatibility of theological and secular subjects in the Greek-Alexandrian Christian School is clearly confirmed by the work and views of Pantaenus, Clement of Alexandria, and Origen.

Pantaenus was at the head of the Christian school of Alexandria in the 170-190s. It is Pantaenus who is mentioned in the sources as the first representative of this school, and for a long period it was called by his name.

Pantaenus determined the direction of the school of Alexandria, which was expressed in the utilization of philosophy and in the solidarity of scientific knowledge with religious teaching. During his tenure as a head of the school, the course of the catechetical school was expressed through exegesis of the Holy Scriptures and conveying the dogmas of faith. He is also credited with teaching a course in Stoicism, as well as works by Pythagoras, Epicurus, Plato, and the Skeptics at the school in Alexandria. The Alexandrian school made a rational understanding of theology and philosophy a priority through the efforts of Pantaenus, and this was accomplished with the unification of faith and knowledge.

His famous disciple Clement of Alexandria combined Biblical and Antique educational principles quite well. In his opinion, the chief teacher is Jesus Christ, Who personifies justice, love, modesty, high spirituality, humanity, and true life. Clement believed that the ideal education implies three hypostases: the mastery of fair habits, the upbringing of the rules of Christian behavior, and the denial of the passions. According to his conception, secular and theological subjects are of equal significance.

A special place in the theological heritage of Clement is devoted to the study of the philosophical problems of faith and knowledge, cognition and teaching. In his opinion, the Greeks took philosophy from the Old Testament, since God owned it, and then the angels gave it to men. It is a great grace that philosophy was given to the Greeks: "Philosophy is a real icon of truth, a divine gift presented to the Greeks" (Stromata, I, 20, 1). Thus, Clement of Alexandria supposes, since philosophy is of divine origin, Christianity could be founded on it, and from a teaching and cognitive point of view, it is a preparatory, i.e., "beginning stage" for obtaining true (Christian) knowledge.

Clement of Alexandria made a special contribution to the improvement of the content of the teaching of the catechetical school. He devoted considerable attention to the importance of studying astronomy and geometry along with philosophy, which was really an unprecedented phenomenon for a catechetical school at that time (Asatiani 2007: 162). According to Clement, "with the help of astronomy, a man rises from the earth in his mind, ascends to heaven, joins the circular rotation, and eternally comprehends both the divine (mysteries) and the mutual consistency (of the universe)" (Stromata, VI, 80, 3). Clement had the same attitude towards geometry, as, in his opinion, it is geometry that "moves you from feelings to the mind" (Stromata, VI, 904).

Clement of Alexandria founded anti-heretical literature, he was the first to academically develop dogmatic and moral theology. The clarification of the relationship between faith and knowledge, the definition of the role and place of philosophy and its compatibility with Christianity can be regarded as his personal merit.

Origen paid particular attention to the compatibility of theological and secular subjects in teaching. He changed the public's attitude to favor civilian subjects, and above all, philosophy, within a short time. Under his influence, the Christian school of Alexandria expanded the area of academic subjects and included secular subjects, in addition to religious subjects. Restrictions on the admission of listeners were also lifted, and the school became open for everybody. With Origen increasing an interest in civil subjects, he encouraged the establishment of an atmosphere of dialogue and respect between Christians and pagans, which his former disciple, St. Gregory the Miracle-Worker, Bishop of Neocaesarea, calls an "intellectual heaven". "Nothing was forbidden for us", the Holy Father remembers, "Nothing was secret, we had the opportunity to listen to every word, be it barbarian or Hellenic, secret or open, divine or human (from St. Gregory's "Address" to Origen)."

Before they began to study the Bible, the disciples of Origen passed a preliminary course, which involved the study of dialectics, physics, mathematics, geometry, and astronomy. After that, philosophy and theology were taught.

Origen's main apologetic work is his book *Against Celsus*, which is a clear example of the polemics between educated Christians and pagans. Both Christians and pagans formulated their ideas freely, indicating that the Christian school of Alexandria was also a hotbed of pluralistic thought.

Origen was not limited in methods of research. If in the interpretation of the Bible he preferred an allegorical method, then in theology he used the Neoplatonic categories. His classical work *About Praying*, where the ways of unity with God are discussed in Neoplatonic categories, confirms exactly this. That is why one can firmly say that Origen tried to give a systematic explanation of the Christian religion through the categories of Hellenic thinking. Clement of Alexandria, whose teaching was inclined towards Gnosticism, set out upon this path earlier. If Clement is a moralist, Origen is a theologian, exegete, apologist, and teacher of ascetic life. Christians are divided into two categories for him: believers and scholars, but every Christian should strive to study the universe.

Clement of Alexandria himself gives such a formulation of the goal of the school of Alexandria. "The acquisition of the basic principles of perfect and purposeful knowledge, which are inextricably linked to higher moral characteristics." Hence it is clear that the school was intended for everyone, and prepared not only clergymen, but Christians in general. At the first stage the school program envisaged the study of such free (general educational) sciences, such as: grammar, dialectics, logic, geometry, astronomy, the natural sciences, and the probability and theory of Pythagorean numbers. Origen also substantiates the need for the creative work of secular writers and points out that when a student is unable to understand the meaning of Holy Scripture and perceive its beauty, he must learn from a secular writer, that is, "to see the sun in the water", and first train his spiritual eyesupon non-Christian writers.

Thus, not only the study of the seven free arts (trivium-quadrivium) was allowed at the early Christian school of Alexandria, but their propaedeutical significance and complete compatibility with the teaching of theological subjects were also acknowledged.

REFERENCES

Asatiani A., 2007, *Essays From the History of Christian Pedagogy*, Vol. 1, Tbilisi.

Gieseler J. C. L., 1831, *Lehrbuch der Kirchengeschichte*, 3-e Ausg. Bonn. [*Church history textbook*]

Losev A. F., 1960, *Alexandrian School//Philosophic Encyclopedia*, Vol. I, Moscow (in Russian)

Prat J.-M., 1843, *Histoire de l'eclectisme alexandrin considere dans sa lutte avec le christianisme*, Vol. I. Lyon. [*History of Alexandrian eclecticism considered in its struggle with Christianity*]

Simone J., 1845, *Historie de l'ecole d'Alexandrie*, V 1–2. Paris. [*History of the school of Alexandria*]

Vacherot E., 1846, *Histoire critique de l'ecole d'Alexandrie*, V. 1–3. Paris. [*Critical History of the School of Alexandria*]

In: Religion and Public Life
Editor: David Muskhelishvili
ISBN: 978-1-53618-904-9
© 2021 Nova Science Publishers, Inc.

Chapter 8

UNDERSTANDING THE PHENOMENON OF HIEROPHANY

Irakli Brachuli[*]

Habilitated Doctor of Philosophy, Associated Professor,
Ivane Javakhishvili Tbilisi State University,
Tbilisi, Georgia

ABSTRACT

"Hierophany" is a fundamental concept of the modern philosophy of myth and religion. The essence of this important phenomenon, more precisely, the concept regarding this phenomenon is explained as manifestation of the sacral and holy.

Keywords: Hierophany, the eternal return of the same, metahistory

"Hierophany" is a fundamental concept of the modern philosophy of myth and religion. It is translated in Georgian as ხატჩენა ("appearance of

---

[*] Corresponding Author's E-mail: irakli.brachuli@tsu.ge.

an icon") or სასწაულცნება ("appearance of a miracle"). This is what the manifestation of the sacral and "holy" in the main forms of culture and human life is called. Rudolph Otto created the term "numinous" to designate it, and it has spread in modern philosophic circles due to Mircea Eliade's works. Below we will try to explain the essence of this important phenomenon, or, more precisely, the concept regarding this phenomenon.

According to Deleuze's observation, the complex of western thinking finds its inner completion in universal pragmatism. Pragmatism is a placing of philosophical thinking within the limits of common sense and everyday suppositions. By this a "great logical illusion" is exposed: the trust in the computational combinatorics of tasks; more precisely, the superstition that thinking is only a double of the common sense supposed from doxa. A question is always copied from supposed or possible answers. A question is based on a preliminary supposition that answers exist in another consciousness. Such questions are: What time is it? When was Caesar born? Deleuze indicates that this point of view loses sight of something that is the most significant in thinking - this is the genesis of the act of thought, i.e., the use of the ability to create thought. We are obliged to believe that ready tasks are given to us in a ready form and they disappear in answers, decisions. This is infantile superstition. Its social precondition leaves us children, underage beings who have not reached adulthood. "This study journal necessarily requires a teacher," who permanently gives tasks and their "solutions," and estimates decisions by scoring them. Suppositions of everyday problems and common sense, i.e., the transfer of natural illusions into philosophical phantoms means placing an idea in the power of identities.

The power of imagination suppresses forces of repetition through images of similarities. This is an essence of Platonism. In accordance with Plato's *Anamnesis*, the copying of what is supposed to be in recollection suppresses the forces of rebirth, eternal return. Thus, a task of modern philosophy - "giving birth to a thought" - emerges. What is this thinking and how should it evolve in the universe?

Difference and repetition are topics similar to the ontology of Nietzsche and Kierkegaard. The universal and necessary permanence of repetition, by which natural and moral laws are characterized, could be only a reflection of an "inner repetition" of deeper and more mysterious vibrations. According to Blessed Augustine and Pascal, "the head is the organ of exchange, and a loving heart is the organ of repetition." "Knowledge is power!" (Bacon) giving us an opportunity to use natural forces, but "repetitions of the heart" are the power of miracles.

Repetition is an awful paradox for the mind, which it must tie with concepts. In an understanding similar to that of Hegel, a concept is a free substance, something that is created, a subject and God, infinite, an endless conclusion containing in itself a mystical omnipotence, that is, a synthesis, the essence of which is created by return and repetition. Synthesis is the process of removing/preserving. Thesis is removed by antithesis. Both thesis and antithesis will again be renewed in synthesis in a removed form. Progress is at the same time a return to the foundation of its own unity. Inner life and the divinity of a concept, its genesis, is a returning motion to its own foundation. Essence and thought are immersed in synthesis, creating a concept, and are preserved in identity. Unity for Hegel is, ultimately, identity.

The basis of identity in the ontology of Deleuze is the substitutability of one thing for another. His social equivalent is a barter exchange. Repetition of such behaviors which are expedient in conditions of irreplaceability. Such conditions are: giving or taking away. If exchange is a criterion of return, the criteria of repetition are giving or taking away. In the lamentation of Job the following idea is underlined: God gave to me, took away from me, and again returned that which is irreplaceable and unchangeable. The offering of Isaac as a sacrifice by Abraham is founded on it. Isaac was God's gift to Abraham (grace), i.e., something different, extreme, without any law (without any general equivalence); the offering of Isaac as a sacrifice was not a barter exchange, but an occurrence (*misteriumtrebedum,* a terrible secret) without any conceptual synthesis, where the classification takes place according to identical signs. This was the celebration of the greatness of difference and a victory against the indifference of identities.

Deleuze and Eliade had not only been drawn together by an "intuitive manner of writing," but also a terminological nomenclature. They had never been co-authors, but both used the word "repetition" as a point of reference for thinking.[1] The trace of their ontologies brings us to Nietzsche, who "again made the myth of eternal return in philosophy relevant." The ontology of cyclic renewal returned to modern thinking, indicating that "knowledge of eternal return is strictly exoteric knowledge." Preachers of such knowledge, "numinous figures," could be hierophants of a charismatic renaissance.

The "Tree of Life" shows the human condition in Deleuze and Eliade's imaginative "meditation." The symbolization of continuous renewal in the Tree of Life with roots and a trunk is marked by Eliade. Its binary double is Deleuze's "tree-rhizome," without a trunk and with decayed roots. Both are models of chaotic consciousness. The most elementary but necessary characteristics for establishing communication by the means of binary pairs are seen in them. After all, the function of a magic situation is precisely to connect binary oppositions, to bring them into a continuum of live perception. In this respect, there is no difference between archaic and modern thinking, both of them consist of the same elements with different ratios (C. Levi-Strauss).

Eliade found the key of religion and myth in a "central mystery," a ritual of the periodical renewal of the universe, which, in his opinion, is the repetition of a sacral story of initial time; myths touch upon a ritual incursion of the sacred (supernatural) into the universe; The things which define and base the human condition in the universe are called hierophanies by Eliade (Eliade, 12).

According to Deleuze, thinking creates concepts and conceptual personages which appear like waves and then plunge...and again return in the "frame of immanence." But "repetitions" do not return identities and similarities. An "eternal return" proceeds from the universe of differences; repetition removes everything which is unnecessary and not new. Thinking

---

[1] The word "repetition" has been reflected even in titles of their books. See Mircea Eliade *The Myth of Eternal Return. Archetypes and Repetition* (1947); J. Deleuze, *Difference et Repetition* (1968).

becomes free from the hegemony of commonality and eternity, beyond the old dichotomies of differences/identities, passes from the vicious cycle of causality, the prose of uniformity, and averageness into the poetry of differences, the vital hierophanies of extraordinariness. The old, positive synthesis of differences/identities changes with a continuous dysfunctional synthesis that is expanded like a rhizome.

"To think philosophically always means to walk on a magical road," says Deleuze. He speaks on the "blessing" of concept. Such a blessing becomes repetitive. Every repetition changes and renews the repeated, and through it differs from the indistinctness of the similar and the simulations of identities. An event of exception acts under this mask in the form of a hierophany.

The behavior of a man thematized by Mircea Eliade is manifested in respect to the sacred in different layers and registers, sometimes secretly and weakly, but the "mythical premises," models of hierophanies are still clearly visible. The repetition of Deleuze and the "initiation" of Eliade are close to each other. Everything returns, as there is nothing equal. Everything swims in its own difference, even in non-coincidence and inequality to itself. What has plunged into indistinctness does not return (Deleuz, 1968, p. 295).

By Eliade's "non-contemporary thinking," a renewal of the human condition will be connected with an attempt of the integration of historical time into a time of cyclicity, i.e., "in the culture of repetitions." It will be dependent on how a man will be able to "include creative spontaneity, the freedom of the creation of his own self" in the archaic ontology of eternal return.

In the 75th paragraph of *Being and Time, Historicity and World History*, Heidegger sums up the existential theory of eternal return. It should be noted that in accordance with Heidegger, the boldness of being-in-itself for death is a return to one's own self, just as Nietzsche's healing of Zarathustra from illness means a return to the same. Repetition is the passing of one's own self to a heritage (tradition). By wholly comprehending finiteness, will we be taken us into the simplicity of our fate. Boldness returned to itself is a repetition, i.e., a return of a former possibility. This is "faithfulness to repetition". Repetition which conveys itself into fate originates from the future. History has its roots in the future. Such repetition retains birth and death in its existence. In such self-transfer time-ecstatic return to his "former" takes place. Birth is brought into existence as a return to a possibility which did not outrun its death.

Faithfulness to boldness (i.e., boldness ready for fear) is awe before the repeated possibility of existence. According to Heidegger, this is "the only existential authority". We read in *Being and Time*: "Boldness constitutes faithfulness of existence to itself. Faithfulness as boldness before fear, is at the same time awe before that only authority who could exist for free existence, i.e., before repeated possibility of existence" (Heidegger, 1989, 578-579).

For an existence living in non-authenticity, repetition is the unification of seconds, ontologically, it is on the contrary. Seconds originate "from a temporality broadened existentially of a former repetition in the future." The word "repetition" makes it easier to understand this very complex situation, which is expressed in a complex way as well. The thought is clearly expressed that a person living in non-authenticity is not able to repeat the former. He/she is blind to eternal return; he/she only collects remnants of the past. The lost past calls him from the present.

The existential theory of the second implies a situation when all times are condensed into "one instance." This is time that infinitely condenses and expands. There are numerous times: a time of writing, a time of a man... Why is one time subjective, but all others - objective, why is one of a certain age and the other is not, why is one the shortest and one the longest? Time can be condensed and but it is not expandable. It might have different shapes. A child who lived only three years did not live less than an 80-year-old man; the lives they have lived are equal in the face of eternity. But their finiteness is of different content and meaning. The synthesis of time and timelessness is an actual infinity. Time should have an end. But what will be after the end? Will it be time again?

Eliade notes that philosophy is associated with ancient mysteries: purification is a necessary condition for philosophical initiation, i.e., the contemplation of higher spheres. The conception of the learning and acquisition of knowledge in Plato's *Phaedo* is organized and motivated by a desire for unity with God, appearing before us like an ecstaticritual initiation... A philosopher is a hierophant.

The aforementioned gives us the opportunity to make a few important observations, if not the possibility of a final presentation of some conclusions. Such a correlation of the hierophanic and energetic aspects of hermeneutics arises in the figure of a superman who expresses the essence of mankind of a new time (M. Heidegger) and plays the role of a guide of philosophical thought in the last hundred years, where there is not only a conflict of interpretations (P. Ricœur), but the conflict of interpretation itself; these aspects (and corresponding concept-personages) can be considered as an acting synthesis and permanent antithesis of philosophical hermeneutics.

The two main contours outlined by Nietzsche in *Superman*: the will for power and the eternal return of the same, were formed as figures to congenitally interpret texts in the romantic hermeneutics of Schleiermacher and Dilthey, whose principle is expressed by the energetic growth of the process of life, unlimited "multiplication," the enrichment of the inner life of thought, inner time, and the formation of super-abundant, super-excessive, super-strong thinking. The hermeneutics of the growth of power and an eternal reverse of the same reveals new possibilities in Husserl's phenomenology, namely, in "eidetic intuition," and in Bergson's hypothesis "of condensed time" (La Dure). Possibilities are revealed in their own way in the figure of technological play, in sophiopraxis, etc. Signs of Nietzsche's "creative nihilism," post-nihilism are seen in them.

The reversion of the energetic paradigm of Dilthey in the theory and practice of understanding can be considered as a postulation of the new ontological possibilities of eternal return which the great hermeneutists of the 20th century, H.G. Gadamer and Paul Ricœur, pointed out. Mircea Eliade and Gil Deleuze's philosophical talks about "difference and repetition" play a reference role for these possibilities on the philosophical plane. The explicit instructions of such differences and repetitions are outlined in Heidegger's *Being and Time*. An existential analysis of "awe to repetition" is implied by it. Postmodern explications of these instructions helped to actualize the narrative regeneration of time and its transformation into something "meta-historical". The returning of modern "street" (public space)'s simulacrum in originalhorde and its rebirth in metahistory is in the same plane.

The figures of a superman in the process of hermeneutic self-determination establish a relation with "ontological throw" (Deleuze), where the idea strives to become a figure and runs away from self-organization in the traditional sense, to identities and artistic perceptions of affects. Correspondingly, "paradigmicity" itself changes. It is freed from "the exemplarity" characteristic to Plato's philosophy. Accordingly, the figures of a superman cannot be relevant either as apocrypha and simulations of Zarathustra, nor as projects of any self-modeling. An accentuation of the following moment seems more important - thought follows ontological singularities ("single events") in the superman's figures, which "are thrown out" and return in different degrees of liberty.

The eternal models characteristic to Plato's philosophy no longer dominate the free differences in the modern hermeneutic situation. This can be seen as a manifestation of the trends of freedom, unknown to the present day, and as an attempt to articulate them philosophically. It is neither necessary, nor possible to again return these "tendencies" to the iron cages of Platonic, Thomistic, or Hegelian type philosophic systems, just as it is neither necessary, nor possible to self-model the essential structures of human existence. The internal ambiguity of hermeneutic concepts indicates that the discovery of a hermeneutic field between some newly revealed ontological possibilities of man and freedom, and holding a dialogue between them is necessary and possible.

REFERENCES

Brachuli, Dura, Zakariadze, 2015; *Philosophy of Religion*, TSU publishing house, Tbilisi, 2015.

Deleuze, 1968: Deleuze Gille, *Différence et Répétition*, Paris, PUF, 1968. [*Difference and Repetition*]

Eliade, 2017: Eliade Mircea, *Myth of Eternal Return. Archetypes and Repetition*, translated by M. Gomelauri, "Alephi," Tbilisi, 2017.

Heidegger, 1989: Heidegger Martin, "*Being and Time,*" translated by Guram Tevzadze, Tbilisi, 1989.

In: Religion and Public Life
Editor: David Muskhelishvili
ISBN: 978-1-53618-904-9
© 2021 Nova Science Publishers, Inc.

Chapter 9

THE CANONICAL FOUNDATIONS FOR THE RESTORATION OF THE GEORGIAN CHURCH'S AUTOCEPHALY

Eldar Bubulashvili[*]

Doctor of Historical Sciences,
Professor at the Theological Academy of Tbilisi,
Main Scientific Worker at Ivane Javakhishvili Institute of History and Ethnology, Member of the Board of the International Centre for Christian Studies at the Orthodox Church of Georgia. Tbilisi, Georgia

ABSTRACT

From the chapter a reader learns that Georgian secular and clerical figures permanently fought for the restoration of the autocephaly of the Georgian Church, which was illegally abolished by the Russian Tsar in the early 19th century. The result of their successful struggle was that on March 12 (25) 1917 the autocephaly of the Georgian Church was restored.

The chapter gives us information on the basis of what ecclesiastical and canonical foundations the Georgian Church regained its

---

[*] Corresponding Author's E-mail: edaribub@yahoo.com.

independence. It is noteworthy that ecclesiastical freedom was soon followed by the restoration of statehood.

Keywords: Georgian Church, autocephaly, Philetism, Catholicos-Patriarch, The interim of the Patriarch, Diocese, Archbishop of Mtskheta-Tbilisi, Metropolitan, Bishop, Russian Church

The Church of Georgia received its autocephaly in the second half of the 5th century. In the 7th-10th centuries, some churches abroad doubted the independence of the Georgian Church, but from a canonical standpoint, its autocephaly was so solid that every attempt at abolishing it ended in failure. The Georgian Church maintained its independence till the end of the 18th century. Initially, its Primate was named Catholicos, later on he was referred to as Patriarch, but in the 10th century he was mentioned as Patriarch of All the East. At the beginning of the 19th century, after the dissolution of the kingdoms of Kartli-Kakheti and Imereti by Russian tsarism, the Georgian Church's autocephaly was abolished per a decision on June 30, 1811 and it became a part of the Russian Holy Synod. The loss of autocephaly was the result of political violence on the part of tsarism and it was fulfilled without any acknowledgement from the Georgian church and its people. The aforementioned act presented a harsh violation of church law.

The results caused by the loss of autocephaly were hard to deal with: it was decreed to perform the Liturgy in church Slavonic, the number of dioceses and Georgian clergy were reduced in number, the Russian Exarchs appointed at the head of the church didn't know Georgian, the Georgian language was forbidden at theological institutions, and ancient Georgian chanting was on the verge of disappearance.

The Georgian public and clergy never put up with the loss of autocephaly and at the beginning of the 19th-20th centuries, they were actively fighting for the restoration of their lost independence. Before the overthrow of its autocracy (February 17, 1917) it was impossible to achieve any good results. Only on March 12/15 at Svetitskhoveli

Cathedral, did the Georgian clergy, headed by Bishop Leonid Okropiridze, declare the restoration of autocephaly in front of 10,000 believers. Bishop Leonid cited the protocol concerning the restoration of Georgian church independence. The original document contains about 600 signatures [The archives of the Georgian Patriarchate. 2-55].

The protocol for the restoration of Georgian church autocephaly is of great interest in light of church canonical law. It reads that the changed political situation, in particular, the formation of a provisional government, promoted the question of the restoration of church autocephaly that had been illegally abolished. The document reads: "Let the autocephalous governance of the Georgian Church be resumed in the shortest possible time" [Protocol 1917: I; Nikoladze 1917:231]. By the same decision, the provisional government of the Georgian Church was chosen at an assembly chaired by Bishop Leonid of Guria-Samegrelo before the election of the Church primate. An executive committee was also formed. Apart from the clergy, secular representatives were elected as members of the new government and Bishop Leonid was chosen to be locum tenens of the Catholicos-Patriarch. Their duty was to manage the affairs of the recently restored, independent Church and fight for the establishment of autocephalous rights before electing the Primate of the church. The new church government introduced the news of the restoration of autocephaly to both the local and Russian provisional governments, the Russian Synod, and former Exarch Plato in written form (Rojdensvenski). Plato didn't recognize the restoration of Georgian Church autocephaly and awaited relevant instructions from Petrograd. The provisional government of the Georgian Church informed the clergy of dioceses extant within Georgia of the decision to stop any relationship with the former Exarch Plato and the synodal office of Georgia-Imereti, get in touch with the presently formed provisional Church government for help, serve the Liturgy in Georgian, and commemorate the name of the temporary head of the Georgian church and locum tenens Catholicos-Patriarch Leonid in their prayers [Georgian Diocese 1917:3].

The news of the restoration of the autocephaly of the Georgian Church was welcomed by both the local provisional government and that of

Petrograd, and they expressed hope, that owing to the existing circumstances, the present issue should be treated within the frame of state legislation.

On March 27, 1917, the provisional Russian government recognized the restoration of the autocephaly of the Georgian Church, but it points out that it"…recognizes Georgian state autocephaly in accordance with its Georgian national character and activities without defining its territorial boundaries". On the basis of the aforementioned decisions, the provisional government allowed the Georgian clergy to work out the proper regulations to be presented to the government for affirmation within the shortest possible time. Before confirming the aforementioned, the Georgian Church government was to follow the old forms of regulations. Yet it was clearly pointed out in the decision that the place of the Church of Georgia in the Russian government in the future should be finally decided at the Founding Assembly [The Georgian Church Autocephaly, 1917:2].

The aforementioned decisions of the provisional Russian government couldn't be accepted by the Georgian Church for the reason that from a church canonical standpoint, it is impossible to form a church in accordance with its national features. This is called phyletism and it had been denounced by the Constantinople Council in 1872 [Papuashvili 2008:430; Dadashkeliani 2011:25-26]. The decision of the provisional government was made due to the fact that the former Exarch Platon had informed the Holy Synod and the head of the provisional Russian government in the name of the Russian clergy and its parishes that their desire was to separate those existing parishes that weren't Georgian yet located on Georgian territory [The Russians of Iber Caucasus and the Autocephaly of the Georgian Church 1917:3].

On March 29, 1917, the provisional government of the Georgian Church had welcomed the fact that the provisional Russian government recognized the restoration of the autocephaly of the Georgian Church in a resolution accepted at a special meeting, but at the same time it emphasized the fact that recognition of Georgian church autocephaly in accordance with its national character was contrary to church laws, "it can't ensure the requirements of the well-being of the Georgian Church and a peaceful co-existence with the Russians living there, as the fighting representatives have a chance to attract Georgians into the Russian Church, thus limiting and humiliating the Georgian Church". The resolution also reads that the autocephaly of the Georgian Church should be recognized on its territorial basis, "on the grounds of the ancient Georgian Catholicate". As for non-Georgian Orthodox believers, they are given "complete freedom for self-determination…in the form of the Georgian…bishopric", the latter - in accordance with church laws - will be subordinated to the Georgian Church. If the Georgians' demands are not taken into consideration, "the Georgian Church keeps the right to address the ecumenical Church stating that it won't take any responsibility for any abnormal events taking place in the country's ecclesiastical life".

According to the resolution, "the Georgian Orthodox Church was to share equal eights with the Russian Orthodox Church" [The Georgian church autocephaly, 1917:3]. The decision reached at the Georgian Church Assembly by the provisional government on March 29, 1917 was sent to the head of the provisional Russian government, the prosecutor of the Holy Synod, and the Caucasian commissariat. The appeal of the provisional government of the Georgian Church was based on Church laws.

The lawful appeal of Georgian theologians was not followed by any response. In order to settle church issues, the provisional Russian government sent a professor of Petersburg University, E. Beneshevich, with relevant instructions in early June, 1917. He met with members of the provisional government of the Georgian Church more than once and also with the Russian clergy and their parishes who were actively at work against autocephaly in Tbilisi. In accordance with the request of the provisional Georgian government, the Georgian Church worked out "some regulations on the rights of the Georgian Church" which were presented to V. Benechenko on April 17, 1917. Consisting of 14 paragraphs, the aforementioned resolution, to some extent, shared the directions of the provisional government. In accordance with the first paragraph, the Georgians of Orthodox parishes were considered to be members of the Georgian Church, both within the jurisdiction of the Georgian Catholicate and beyond it. In a note to the same paragraph, it is pointed out that the Abkhazian and Ossetian populations of Eurasia were allowed to become members of the Georgian Church in accordance to a wish explained by their historical coexistence. In accordance with the second paragraph, Orthodox believers, but not Georgians, were considered to not be members of the Georgian Church. The Georgian clergy were obliged to meet their religious requirements if requested. In return, the non-Georgian clergy was told to act the same way towards Georgian parishes, but the Church had no right to make them members of their parish. In a note to the same paragraph, an applicant had no right to express his religious requirements in his native language.

The following paragraph reads that the Georgian Church consists of dioceses and parishes. Their number was to be fixed in accordance with specially certified lists. According to the resolution, the Primate of the Georgian Church was to be referred to as "Archbishop of Mtskheta and Tbilisi, Catholicos-Patriarch of All Georgia". The latter was to be elected, by a direct, equal, general, and secret ballot.

The introduction of an electoral system in the draft resolution could be explained by the well-rooted democracy in society after the fall of tsarism. In accordance with the resolution, the Catholicos could be elected by both ecclesiastical and secular representatives, but before being consecrated he was to be approved by secular authorities. The residence of the primate of the Church was supposed to be in Tbilisi. He was allowed to have correspondence with autocephalous churches and governmental institutions. The Catholicos-Patriarch and his board of Catholicoses were allowed to work out governmental regulations of the Church based on church laws and they shouldn't have been opposed to the state legislation. According to the resolution, the Georgian Church in the Russian state was to share equal rights with the Russian Orthodox Church. In the following paragraph of the resolution, it is stated that all the institutions under the Catholicate were supposed to be financed from the budget of the former exarchate until the settlement all religious issues. The primate of the Georgian church was to settle the following affairs: the formation of monetary accountancy, its presentation to the relevant state structures, and its management. According to the draft resolution, the Georgian Church was considered to be a legal entity and it was given the right to buy, manage, and sell. All property of the former exarchate was declared to belong to the Georgian Church except the property of non-Georgian parishes. A separate paragraph was dedicated to theological institutions of the Georgian Church that were supposed to share equal rights with Russian theological institutions in Russia. In the final paragraph it was stated that all the institutions of the Georgian Catholicate including theological ones were to conduct all proceedings in Georgian. All the aforementioned paragraphs except the first one are formed from the standpoint of ecclesiastical law. In accordance with some paragraphs of the resolution, the influence of democracy after the overthrow of the monarchy is clearly seen. Because of the first paragraph, the provisional government of the Georgian Church added an amendment stating that they are forced to take into account the directions of the provisional government in recognizing autocephaly on a national basis "without taking any responsibilities on its part before history and the Ecumenical Church", for introducing such an anti-canonical principle causing practical discomfort and also opening the way for the phyletism that had been banned by the Georgian Orthodox Church [Resolution of the Georgian Church... Rights, 1917:3]. V. Beneshevich fully accepted this aforementioned resolution and wired it for approval to the provisional government in Petrograd. He assured the Georgian public that he would support the restoration of the autocephaly of the Georgian Church on his return to Petrograd in accordance with its territorial markers. But in reality, V. Beneshevich was not sincere. It appeared that he was against the restoration of the autocephaly of the Georgian Church. He warned Petrograd against approving the resolution before his return [Tsintsadze 2001:192].

The provisional government was not in a hurry to approve this resolution. Telegrams addressed to the provisional government and to Leonid, locum tenens of the Catholicos-Patriarch, arrived from different parts of Georgia, Russian towns, and abroad. They all expressed their negative attitude regarding the provisional government and Prof. Beneshevich's visit.

Immediately after receiving autocephaly, the provisional government of the Georgian Church came to settle organizational issues and liturgy was served in accordance with old Georgian traditions. The clergy, servants of the church, and church singers were given relevant instructions. Annunciation Day, Palm Sunday, and Easter were solemnly celebrated. On May 1, a solemn liturgy was held on the commemoration day of St. Queen Tamar. Soon after the declaration of the independence of the Georgian Church, the Russian clergy raised their voices against it and they were followed by the Russian dioceses. It should be noted that non-Georgians such as the Abkhazians, Ossetians, Armenians, and the Udi supported the Georgian Church's independence. The Udi went so far as to ask for permission to become a part of the Georgian Church. On March 30, 1917, an article appeared in the newspaper "Sakartvelo" (Georgia). The article was written by some non-Georgian teachers, mostly Russians, from theological institutions "heartily wishing the Georgian Church free and independent development for its future success in science and religious thinking" [The Autocephaly of the Georgian Church, 1917:3]. The restoration of autocephaly was also supported by a newspaper published in Petrograd "Petrograd Structures", where, beginning at the end of the 19th century, some interesting publications had appeared concerning the Georgian church. The same newspaper often published letters by N. Durnovo, who was a great supporter of the Georgians. In them she criticized the tsarist church policy. N. Durnovo was against the provisional government recognizing the autocephaly of the Georgian Church in accordance with its national character and supported the idea of church government in accordance with its territorial features. Autocephaly was sided by the Archbishop of Novgorod, former rector of Moscow Theological Academy, PhD, and a former member of the state board. Arsen (Stadninski) and Bishop Andre (Ukhtomski) of Ufa were also among the supporters. The latter was archpriest of the Sokhumi Diocese in 1911-1913. In his article published in the newspaper "Новоевремя" he claims that "restoration of the autocephaly of the Georgian Church was an act of justice and a great event in connection with the Orthodox Church" [Tsintsadze, 2001:226].

Per the initiative of the opposing Russian clergy at the assembly held in Tbilisi, on May 22, 1917, it was proposed to found a separate church government in Transcaucasia. On the basis of their appeal due to the proposal of the prosecutor, the provisional regulations of the Russian Church were fixed. These regulations would mean the establishment of a Caucasian Exarchate that would oversee non-Georgian parishes extant within the boundaries of the former Exarchate. Tbilisi was destined to become the residence of the Exarch of the Caucasus. He was endowed with the title of Metropolitan of Tbileli and Caucasian Exarch [Egorov 1917:28]. The aforementioned decision of the provisional government was a gross violation of church law and was canonically contrary to the governing body of the Georgian Church. All this clearly shows that the provisional government had first approved a temporary resolution that had been worked out by the Holy Synod concerning Russian parishes in the Caucasus, after which it had worked out a temporary resolution concerning the Georgian Church that was supposed to be based on the resolution worked out by the provisional government [Egorov, 1917:28]. On July 25, 1917, the provisional government of Russia approved the conditions of some temporary regulations of the Georgian Orthodox Church in Russia. Some passages from these regulations worked out earlier were brought about in an altered form. The Georgian delegation sent to Petersburgby the provisional government of the Georgian Church failed to bring about any good results. Among the members of the delegation were Bishop Anton (Giorgadze), Archpriest M. Kelenjeridze, etc. and those Georgians who were actively at work in the Russian government.

The three paragraphs of the resolution signed by Minister-Chairman A. Kerenski andProsecutor A. Kartashev are of a general character, with the first paragraph confirming the regulations of the temporary resolution. In the second paragraph a special commission was formed consisting of members approved by the provisional government. The commission was supported in defining which part of the exarchate property was to be confiscated. In the final paragraph of the resolution it was stated that before founding the Ministry of Religion, the prosecutor of the synod enjoyed the same rights with the Church of Georgia as it had enjoyed with the Exarchate. Thus, according to this final paragraph, the Church of Georgia had become dominated by the Russian Synod once again, thus causing dissatisfaction on the part of the Georgian public and clergy.

As for the approved resolution, the draft resolution wasn't approved in the altered form. It underwent some basic changes to make clear the idea of the autocephaly of the Georgian Church in accordance with nationality. The first part of the resolution corresponds to the relevant paragraph of the draft resolution, according to which a member of a parish was supposed to be an Orthodox Georgian within the boundaries of the Russian state. Paragraphs 3 and 4 are completely relevant to the paragraph of the draft resolution concerning the fulfillment of religious requirements and the governance of dioceses and parishes. In accordance with the second paragraph, the people of Abkhazian and Ossetian nationalities could choose to become members of the Georgian Church if they so desired. In the publications of the Georgian press, people of Ossetian nationality were excluded and they were substituted by "Trans-Caucasian parishes". In some places only the Abkhazian people are mentioned causing some misunderstanding. In Russian publications, the Ossetians from the Trans-Caucasus are clearly pointed out ("Закавказскихосетин") [Egorov, 1917:36]. In accordance with the approved resolution, the Primate of the Georgian Church is not just mentioned as Catholicos Patriarch of All Georgia, Archbishop of Mtskheta-Tbilisi as it had been stated in the draft project, but as "Archbishop of All Georgians and Mtskheta". In accordance with this resolution, non-Georgian Orthodox believers weren't considered to be part of the legislation of the Georgian Church. Tbilisi was excluded from the titles of the Primate of the Georgian Church. The newspaper "Sakartvelo" stated: "The Georgian national conscience couldn't put up with such a violation of the law and the humiliation and in an address to the Synod it states that it no longer has the right to interfere with the affairs of the autocephalous Georgian Church [Confirmation of Autocephaly, 1917:2]. In accordance with paragraph 8 of the resolution, the Primate of the Georgian Church had his residence in Tbilisi. In the resolutions published in the Georgian press nothing is mentioned on the matter, it is attested only in the Russian sources published in Russian [Egorov,

1917:36]. It is acceptable to have the residence of the Primate of the Church in Tbilisi. Yet Tbilisi is not mentioned among the titles of the Primate of the Georgian Church. Even more, by a decision of the provisional government on July 11, 1917, the non-Georgian archpriest of the Trans-Caucasus is to be called the Metropolitan of Tbilisi and his residence is in Tbilisi. The aforementioned refers to phyletism. According to Church law it is forbidden to have the residences of two similar archpriests of the same confession in one and the same place. In accordance with the approved resolution the Catholicos-Patriarch's contact with autocephalous churches abroad is limited. He could do that through the Ministry of Foreign Affairs of Russia. Paragraphs 9-13 of the resolution are in full harmony with the draft resolution, which deals with the finances of the Catholicate, his recognition as a legal entity, the issues of the status of theological institutions, their operation and management in the Georgian language. The final, confirmed 14th paragraph not mentioned in the draft resolution obliges the Church to register marriages in accordance with civil laws.

An analysis of the approved resolution shows that the provisional government did not only fail to meet the requirements of the Georgian clergy and the public but introduced such changes in the basic paragraphs of the resolution that showed more vividly the phyletism so strongly denounced by the church. The aforementioned resolution was devoid of any canonical foundations and expressed the will of the Russian government [Dadashkeliani, 2011:26]. The Georgian clergy and public again expressed their dissatisfaction with the resolution. As seen from its title, the aforementioned resolution was temporary. It was in effect until the founding assembly that was to be convened in January, 1918. It was supposed to accept some concessions in order to regulate the place of the autocephalous Georgian Church in the Russian state. In spite of the approved resolution, the provisional government of the Georgian Church wasn't going to manage church affairs in accordance with it.

On August 15, 1917 with the aim of establishing Church canon, Leonid, the locum tenens of the Catholicos-Patriarch and the Bishop of Guria-Samegrelo, was appointed as the Tbileli Metropolitan, a position that had been recently restored by the Synod of Russia after having been abolished a century ago. The aforementioned decision was a reasonable step made by the Georgian Church in accordance with Church legislation. The Exarch of the Caucasus couldn't become the Tbileli Metropolitan, but the Synod didn't mind this fact and the former exarch Platon was appointed as the Tbileli Metropolitan on the same day. On August 23 of the same year, the Georgian Church occupied the building of the former Exarchate in a peaceful way. True, there followed a wave of dissatisfaction on the part of the Holy Synod, but this building had been bought by the Georgian clergy in the middle of the 19th century.

The declaration of autocephaly played a big role in the formation of church organizational structure issues. On September 8-17, 1917, the first Church Assembly was held in Tbilisi. Representatives of all parishes from different parts of Georgia, both secular and clerical deputies chosen by secret ballot, participated in its work. New dioceses were established per the decision of the Assembly. The new archpriests were chosen, Kyrion II (Sadzaglishvili) was chosen as Catholicos-Patriarch by direct and secret ballot. The recently chosen CatholicosKyrion II sent some epistles concerning the restoration of the autocephaly of the Georgian Church to Patriarchs of the East, the Pope of Rome, and the Catholicos of Armenia. The Assembly approved the governmental resolution based on ecclesiastic canonical law. It is noteworthy that preparation for the church assembly and the issues discussed there were settled on the basis of democratic principles, which could be explained by the fact that after the February revolution of 1917, democracy became widespread in the former Russian Empire. The provisional government of the Georgian Church was trying to establish democratic principles under the influence of the secular government but there should have been no violation of canonical norms in doing so.

In the adopted resolution at the first Church Assembly concerning the governance of the Church, the principle of church establishment confirmed by the Holy Synod wasn't taken into consideration. In accordance with the new resolution for church governance, the structural establishment of the Georgian Church was carried out in accordance with its territorial principles. Non-Georgian parishes appeared under its legislation together with Georgian ones. The Primate of the Church of Georgia was referred to as the Bishop of Mtskheta and Catholicos-Patriarch of all Georgia, whose residence was in Tbilisi. In 1919, after abolishing the position of Metropolitan, the Catholicos-Patriarch was considered to be the Archbishop of Mtskheta-Tbilisi. By decision of the Church Assembly, the Georgian Church was established in accordance with canonical laws. The provisional government and the Russian Church, which had been restored with full rights after the Church Assembly in Russia, expressed their dissatisfaction with this resolution. With the help of the Exarchs of the Caucasus stationed in Tbilisi, they openly conducted their anti-church policy. Even after restoring the statehood of Georgia (on May 26, 1918), the Exarch of the Caucasus stationed in Tbilisi carried out a policy directed against the Georgian state, due to which it was abolished in February, 1920. By a decision of the Democratic State of Georgia, Exarchate members had to leave the country's territory [Bubulashvili, 2008:33]. Earlier, on December 29, 1917, the Russian Metropolitan Tikhon (Beljaev) sent a threatening epistle to the archpriests, accusing them of violating Church laws. On August 5, 1919, an argumentative response based on Church law was sent to the recently chosen Patriarch Tikhon of Moscow and all Russia in the name of the Catholicos of Georgia, Leonid Okropiridze (1919-1921). There was no communication between these two countries for a long time and only in 1943 did the Russian Church accept the restored autocephaly of the Georgian Church and its canonical basis. Communication between the two countries was then restored [Bubulashvili, 2003:54-55].

Later on, the future independence of the Georgian Church was greatly influenced by the restoration of Georgian statehood. True, the atheistic government of Social-Democrats was deprived of any warm feelings towards the Georgian Church but after the declaration of the country's independence, Church legislation sided with that of the state and parishes consisted of both Georgians and non-Georgians. In this case, the recently sovietized Russian government and its Church had no right to interfere in the internal affairs of the Georgian Church.

REFERENCES

Autocephaly of the Church of Georgia 1917 a: Georgia 1917, N 71, 30 March.
Autocephaly of the Church of Georgia 1917 b: Georgia 1917, N 72, 31 March.
Bubulashvili. (2003). Bubulashvili E. *Some issues of communication between the Church and State*, 1918-1921, Logosi, N 1, Tbilisi.
Bubulashvili. (2008). Bubulashvili E. 2008, *The Orthodox Church of Georgia*, Tbilisi.
Dadashkeliani. (2011). Dadashkeliani I, 2011, *autocephaly of the Georgian Orthodox Church* (Canonical Legislative Analysis), Tbilisi.
Eparchy of Georgia. (1917). Georgia, 1917, N 62, 18 March.
Егоров. (1917). Егоров В. 1917. *К истории провозглашения Грузинами автокефалии своей в 1917 году, Москва*. [*On the history of the proclamation of their autocephaly by Georgians in 1917, Moscow*]
Human Rights of the Church of Georgia, resolution. (1917). Georgia, 1917, N 90, 21 April.
Nikoladze. (1918). Nikoladze N. 1918, *History of the Church of Georgia*, Kutaisi.
Papuashvili. (2008). Papuashvili N. 2008, *Korneli Kekelidze at the First Church Council and Atributation issues of two canonical documents of the Council, in Christian-archeological search, I, Tbilisi*.
Patriarchal Archives of Georgia, *Patriarchal Archives of Georgia*, N 645.
Protocol. (1917). "Georgia" 1917 N 59, 15 March.
The Russians of Trans-Caucasus and Autocephaly of the Church of Georgia, 1917, N 71, 30 March.
Tsintsadze. (2001). Tsintsadze K. 2001, *From my recollection*, Tbilisi.

In: Religion and Public Life
Editor: David Muskhelishvili
ISBN: 978-1-53618-904-9
© 2021 Nova Science Publishers, Inc.

Chapter 10

THE STRUGGLE FOR THE RECOGNITION AND ACKNOWLEDGMENT OF THE AUTOCEPHALY OF THE GEORGIAN CHURCH – 20TH CENTURY

*Tamar Meskhi**
Ilia State Univeristy, G. Tsereteli Institute of Oriental Studies, Researcher, Doctor of Philology, Tbilisi, Georgia

ABSTRACT

The leaders of the Georgian Orthodox Church took advantage of the state changes in Russia and on March 12, 1917, restored the autocephaly of the Georgian Church, which was illegally abolished by the Russian Church in 1811. In October of the same year, the Catholicos-Patriarch of All Georgia, Kirion II, informed the Orthodox Churches of Constantinople and other Eastern Churches (of Alexandria, Antioch, and Jerusalem) about this important event and asked for their support. Since the Georgian Church has not received any reply letters, the Georgian ecclesiastical and scientific community still holds the view that the

---

* Corresponding Author's E-mail: meskhi_tamara@yahoo.gr.

restoration of the autocephaly of the Georgian Church has not been recognized by any of the Orthodox Churches.

Research has shown that this view is incorrect. In November 1919, on the instructions of the Synod of the Church of Constantinople, Metropolitan Chrysanthos of Trabzon (later, 1938-1940, Archbishop of Greece) visited the Georgian Church. He presented an extensive report card to the Synod of the Church of Constantinople (published in the magazine Ἐκκλησιαστικὴ Ἀλήθεια, 1/8/1920). In the report card Metropolitan Chrysanthos of Trabzon had the request to the Church of Constantinople to have the role of conciliator between the Georgian and Russian churches in order to return to the Georgian Church the status it had a hundred years ago.

Unfortunately, the Church of Constantinople failed to act as a mediator. Its inaction and silence, as well as of other Orthodox Churches, is explained not by ignoring the Georgian Church, but by the historical events that took place in the world caused by the First World War.

Keywords: Georgian Church, acknowledgement of autocephaly, Patriarch

The autocephaly of the Georgian Church and the patriarchal title of its head repeatedly became a matter of dispute with the Patriarchates of Russia and Antioch. These issues re-emerged on the agenda of the Georgian Church during the 1970s. Catholicos-Patriarch Ilia II officially demanded from the Ecumenical Patriarchate recognition of the autocephaly of the Georgian Orthodox Church, which it had from ancient times, as well as documents confirming this act.

The attempts of the head of the Georgian Church yielded some results. On March 4, 1990, at the celebration of Orthodoxy in Constantinople (Istanbul) the relevant documents were passed to the Catholicos-Patriarch of Georgia, Ilia II. But it was not so easily achievable. Meetings and negotiations went on for twelve years (1978-1990). Several official representatives of the Constantinople Church visited the Georgian Church during this period. I was fortunate to be a part of these talks and see everything, as I translated all these talks and corresponded with the

Patriarchate of Constantinople.[1] But now I will focus your attention on a completely different matter.

One could firmly say that the question of recognition of autocephaly would never have been on the agenda of the Georgian Church, had the Russian Church not abolished it. The explanatory paper of Metropolitan Chrisanthos of Trebizond (1913-1938; 1938-1940, later - Archbishop of Athens and All Greece), which he presented to the Holy Synod of the Constantinople Patriarchate on July 15, 1920, and which was published in the official journal «Ἐκκλησιαστικὴ Ἀλήθεια» of the Ecumenical Patriarchate the same year, gives us the possibility to say this.

The explanatory paper of Metropolitan Chrisanthos refers to the role of St. Nino in the conversion of the Georgians. The metropolitan does not have doubts concerning the autocephaly of the Georgian Church, but thinks that the Georgian Church had to have obtained autocephaly about 1054. Besides, it is described how selflessly the autocephalous Church of Georgia had defended Christianity for eight centuries until July 11, 1811, when the Russian Church abolished it and appointed an exarch to it. It is also noted how the restoration of the autocephaly of the Georgian Church took place on March 12 (25), 1917 and what was the reaction of the Russian Church to this.

Now, I would like to draw your attention to the final part of his explanatory paper, where he describes in what state the Georgian Church was when he saw it in November, 1917, and how he imagined a way out of the situation:

"On June 14, 1917, the Russian Church passed the law in a hurry concerning the issues on the management of the Russian Church in the Caucasus. Its own representative in Tbilisi is Theophylact, Bishop of Elisabethpol, in the jurisdiction of whom are Russians living in the Caucasus and everybody else who wishes it. *Thus, the two national independent churches operate uncanonically in this geographic area...* In my humble opinion," continues the Metropolitan, "a *serious and*

---

[1] In connection with those negotiations and obtaining those charters, see: Tamar Meskhi, "And ye shall know the truth, and the truth shall make you free", *Journal "Jvari Vazisa"*, 1990, #3, 18-24; reprinted: 2009, # 1, 177-186.

conciliatory interference of the Constantinople Church, which has a superiority (that during the history turned out to be successful in such extreme situations both for Russian and Georgian Churches), *will settle this misunderstanding. It will assure that the Holy Synod of the Russian Church recognizes the Georgian Church in the status which it had one hundred years ago, as an autocephalous Church, of course, in the case if both sides have this good will, especially now, when the faithful Georgian nation had restored its state status.*"[2]

Thus, it is clearly seen from the excerpt that the question of the autocephaly of the Georgian Church was not at all controversial for the Metropolitan of Trebizond, moreover, Chrisanthos urged the Ecumenical Patriarchate to play the role of conciliator between the Russian and Georgian Churches, to restore the status of the Georgian Church in the limits that it had had before 1811.

Unfortunately, when the Georgian Church, under the leadership of His Holiness Ilia II, conducted negotiations with the Church of Constantinople regarding autocephaly, the fact of the Metropolitan of Trabzon's visit to the Georgian Church, as well as his explanatory paper, were unknown to us. The Greek side also did not pay attention to this fact.

Some might comprehend the point of view presented in the explanatory letter as the point of view of one metropolitan of the Constantinople Patriarchate, or as an academic paper. For the right assessment, we should first recall the era when this paper was written, and then how and why it was written.

Metropolitan Chrisanthos arrived in Batumi on November 3, 1919. The purpose of his visit to Georgia was to get acquainted with the living conditions of the Pontic Greeks and, if possible, help them.

As it is known, at the beginning of the First World War, the Turks and Kurds began to oppress Greeks living in the Ottoman Empire and made them leave their homes and settle in the Caucasus or the southern regions of Russia. After the revolution of 1917, the Bolsheviks became hostile to the Greeks, as Greece became an ally of the Entente countries and took

---

[2] Ἄρθρακαὶ Μελέται Χρυσάνθου, ἈρχιεπισκόπουἈθηνῶντοῦἀπὸΤραπεζοῦντος (1911-1949), ὑπόΓ. Ν. Τασούδη (βιβλίοντρίτον), Ἀθῆναι, 1997, 305-306.

part in the military operations on their side to drive the Bolsheviks out of Ukraine. That is why most Greeks moved to Georgia in search of refuge. But Georgia itself was not in an enviable state. The independence of Georgia hung by a thread and waited for help from Europe.[3]

The Greek government found a way out of the situation in providing assistance to refugees on the spot and conducted their selective repatriation. That is why in June, 1912, it sent a special diplomatic mission headed by the famous Greek writer Nikos Kazantzakis to Georgia. On August 11, 1919, the first ship with Pontic Greeks on the deck went to Greece. N. Kazantzakis also went with them, but members of the mission stayed in Georgia and continued their work under the leadership of Janis Stavridakis.

On November 29, 1919, J. Stavridakis got a telegram from Constantinople in which the Highest Commissar of Greece, E. Kanellopoulos instructed him to find Metropolitan Chrisanthos, being in Georgia, and to convey to him the special task of the Holy Synod of the Ecumenical Patriarchate: 1. To see in what condition the Georgian Church was, which had just restored autocephaly; 2. "On behalf of the Ecumenical Patriarchate and the corresponding respect of the Georgian Church," to assure the authorities of the Georgian Church of the favorable attitude of the Ecumenical Patriarchate regarding them. And to explain the silence of the Patriarchate by delays in correspondence and the sudden resignation of the Patriarch of Constantinople.[4]

Naturally, a question arises: what letter and "silence" are mentioned in the telegram?

The fact is that in October, 1917, Catholicos-Patriarch of all Georgia Kirion II sent some letters to the Patriarchates of Constantinople and other Orthodox Churches (Alexandria, Antioch, and Jerusalem) through which he informed them of the restoration of the autocephaly of the Georgian

---

[3] Despite this, the government of Georgia allocated 2,000,000 rubles to help refugees regardless of their nationalities. Το Έργον των Αποστόλων του Υπουργείου Περιθάλψεως» (Πόντος, Κωνσταντινούπολης, Σμύρνη, Μακεδονία), Εν Αθήναις 1920, 27.

[4] Synod instructed the leader of the diplomatic mission working in Georgia J. Stavridakis to do the same, ΒιογραφικαίαναμνήσειςτουΧρυσάνθουΑρχιεπισκόπουΑθηνώντουαπό Τραπεζούντος, 1881-1949, Αθήναι 1970, 272.

Orthodox Church and asked them for assistance and joint prayers. Unfortunately, an answer did not come from any patriarchate. And the Russian Church spread false epistles on behalf of the Patriarchs of Constantinople and Antioch, as if they had advised Georgians to submit to the Russian Patriarchate.[5]

In reality, the silence of the eastern Orthodox Churches was due to the international situation of that period and tragic events in the Georgian Church: Catholicos-Patriarch of Georgia Kirion II was treacherously killed some months after sending the letter (on June 27, 1918). The next Catholicos-Patriarch, Leonide, was elected only on February 23, 1919. During all this time there were unrest and confrontation in the Georgian Church. The murders of the supporters of Kirion were continued.[6] It is clear that the Orthodox Churches of the East observed the processes taking place in the Georgian Church and did not hurry with an answer. Supposedly, they waited for the situation to calm down in the Georgian Church, but at this time the situation worsened in their Churches.

The Ottoman Empire was on the verge of destruction. This also affected the Orthodox Churches on its territories. The main concern for

---

[5] "*...I don't acknowledge the independent Georgian Church and I even cannot do it as you, Orthodox Georgians, have been under the protection of the Russian Church for more than 100 years, (...) your autocephaly is possible only after agreement with the Russian Church... I paternally advise you to listen to your shepherd*"(Russian Patriarch is implied - T. M.)" - as if the Patriarch of Constantinople German V said it, and on behalf of the Patriarch of Antioch and of all the East, Gregorius IV, such a letter was distributed: "*Silly Georgians! Have you forgotten for how many years you enjoyed peace and quiet under the protection of the Russian Orthodox Church? You have never been autocephalous. You've always had discords and turmoil, and we had to settle everything for your benefit, but when we became weak and were not able to assist you, then the Shepherd of Shepherds raised the Candle of the North - the new protector for all Orthodox, including you. And now when this state has become diseased, you, like ungrateful children, rose against the Russian Church. How did you think that we would sympathize with you and would be your accomplices in your illegal exaltation? We advise you to change your mind and address your Holy Fatherwith regret - Patriarch of all Russia Tikhon, our beloved brother in Christ and prayer with us*", K. Georgievskiy [K. Tsintsadze], About an Archpastoral Forgery, "Грузия", 1, II, N 5 (in Russian); Kalistrate Tsintsadze, Preaches and Speeches, prepared for publication by N. Papuashvili, Tbilisi, 2014, pp. 216-218 (in Georgian).

[6] In 1918, Metropolitan Anton of Kutaisi was poisoned (by his own son-in-law), on October 15th the same year priest Timothe Bakuradze (the head of the pre-election agitation of Kirion II in the provinces) was killed at his house, monks Mirian (Bekauri) and Germogen were killed in Armazi Monastery on June 6, 1919... S. Vardosanidze, Catholicos-Patriarch of Georgia, His Holiness and Beatitude Kirion II (1855-1918), Tbilisi, 2014, p. 126.

them was to save the Church and the flock. As for the Patriarchate of Constantinople, in addition to the aforementioned problems, Patriarch German V (1913-1918) resigned on October 31, 1918.[7] The Holy Synod of the Church of Constantinople asked the Metropolitan of Trebizond to explain exactly this situation.

Metropolitan Chrisanthos fulfilled the task of the Synod. He remarks in his memoirs: "I have visited the Georgian Church several times. I have written a lengthy explanatory letter for the Ecumenical Patriarchate, in which I support the autocephaly of the Georgian Church. I have visited the Prime-Minister and the Ministry of Foreign Affairs of Georgia. Both clergymen and politicians are very pleasant. I also had to protect them from the propaganda of the Catholics, which was very active. That is why I asked the Georgian Church to establish a close contact with the Ecumenical Patriarchate."[8]

Since the explanatory letter of Metropolitan Chrisanthos was published in the official organ of the Ecumenical Patriarchate, we should suppose that the Synod of the Constantinople Church supported the point of view of Chrisanthos, but we could not find out yet if it had reacted to it, i.e., if it had written any official letter to the Russian Church.

In any case, within just a year, Georgia lost its independence on February 25, 1921. The Georgian Church, which turned out to be a part of the atheistic empire, not only could not think about the restoration of autocephaly, but was limited in correspondence with other Orthodox churches.

The Church of Constantinople was not in any better situation. When Metropolitan Chrisanthos arrived in Georgia (in November 1919), Constantinople was occupied by English and French troops. The emptied patriarchal throne was protected by two sub-units of the Greek army. In the same year 1919, Mustafa Kemal-Pasha (Ataturk) founded the Turkish

---

[7] English and German troops entered Constantinople in 1918. That day the elderly Patriarch of Constantinople German conducted a funeral service for the people who died in the war. Some provocateurs caused riots in the church. The Patriarch had a heart attack and fell down unconscious in the church. Some days later he resigned. In December, 1920, German V died.

[8] ΒιογραφικαὶἈναμνήσειςτοῦΧρυσάνθουἈρχιεπισκόπουἈθηνῶντοῦἀπὸΤραπεζούντος (1881-1949), Ἀθῆναι 1970, 272.

National Congress, which subdued all of Turkey in 1919-1922, drove out the Greeks and Armenians, regained Constantinople in 1923, and laid the foundations of the Turkish Republic. The Ecumenical Patriarchate found itself facing new challenges - it had to settle relations with the new government.

The First World War created problems for Patriarchates of Antioch and Jerusalem as well. In December 1917, Palestine was occupied by England. The so-called "Arab problem"[9] again worsened in the Patriarchate of Jerusalem, the purpose of which was the abolition of status quo of the Patriarchate of Jerusalem.

In 1918, French troops entered Syria. One part of the country was annexed to the Kingdom of Iraq, and the second one was controlled by the French Mission (since 1920 - The League of Nations), that contributed to the strengthening of the Catholics; Protestants also spread; the proselytism of the Orthodox began. The majority of the population of Syria was Arab Muslims, Turks, and Druze. Judeans also lived there. And what is more, Christians had 8 patriarchates in Syria and Lebanon by that time.[10] The historical Orthodox Patriarchate of Antioch was on the brink of extinction.

In a word, because of historical cataclysms in the world, the recognition of the autocephaly of the Georgian church was postponed for 70 years.

Metropolitan Maximus of Sardis (1965), Professor of the University of Athens V. Phidas (1980), Metropolitan Damaskinos of Switzerland (1986), and others devoted special studies to the history of the Georgian Church and its autocephaly. Neither Greek clergymen, nor historians reject the fact that the Georgian Church was autocephalous. But in their point of view, the Georgian Church obtained autocephaly in the middle of the

---

[9] This problem was provoked by the Pan-Slav movement, which was organized by the Russians in the second half of the 19th century. His goal was to drive the Greeks out of Syria and Palestine and awaken chauvinistic feelings among Arab-speaking Greeks and other Christians in order to capture the Jerusalem church. In the beginning, England supported the Greeks, but later tried to abolish the status quo existing in the Holy Land in every possible way.

[10] Κονιδάρης Γερ. Ι., Ἀντιόχεια, Θρησκευτικὴ καὶἨθικὴἘγκυκλοπαίδεια, τ. 2ος, Ἀθῆναι, 1963, 903.

11th century[11] and not in the 5th century, as is accepted in Georgian church tradition. It was the recording of this date that became the subject of controversy at the talks that the Georgian Church, led by His Holiness Ilia II, conducted with the Ecumenical Patriarchate. Finally, the Patriarchate of Constantinople reacted with understanding to the tradition of the Georgian Church and wrote down in the document as follows:

> "We, according to the decision of the Synod and, enlightened by the Holy Spirit, declare the Holy Church of Georgia with the same self-governing structure and organization which it has had since ancient times and which is also substantiated by Balsamon who wrote: ...They say that at the time of His Holiness Peter, the Patriarch of the divine great city of Antioch, the Synod adopted a decreestating that the Georgian Church would be free and autocephalous."

Thus, the receipt on March 4, 1990 of documents substantiating the autocephaly of the Georgian Church was a great victory for the Georgian Church. And henceforth no one can encroach upon it.

REFERENCES

Georgievskiy K. [K. Tsintsadze], *About an Archpastoral Forgery*, "Грузия," 1, II, N 5 (in Russian).

Meskhi, T. *Journal "Jvari Vazisa,"* 1990, N 3, 18-24; reprinted: 2009, N 1, pp. 177-186.

Tsintsadze, Kalistrate. *Sermons and Speeches*, Prepared for publication by N. Papuashvili, Tbilisi, 2014.

Tsintsadze, Kalistrate. Works in Two Volumes, V. II, *Historical Information on the Autocephaly of the Georgian Church: Mcignobroba Kartuli*, 10, 2010.

Vardosanidze, S. *Catholicos-Patriarch of All Georgia, His Holiness and Beatitude*, Kirion II (1855-1918), Tbilisi, 2014.

---

[11] This view was also expressed by some Georgian researchers, including Kalistrate Tsintsadze Catholicos-Patriarch of All Georgia. See: K. Tsintsadze, V. II, Historical Information on the Autocephaly of the Georgian Church: Mtsignobroba Kartuli 10, 2010, pp. 7-136.

Χρυσάνθου, Ἀρχιεπισκόπου Ἀθηνῶν τοῦἀπό Τραπεζούντος (1911-1949), Ἄρθρα καὶ Μελέται, ὑπό Γ. Ν. Τασούδη (βιβλίον τρίτον), Ἀθῆναι, 1977. [Chrysanthos, Bishop of Athens touapo Trapezountos (1911-1949), article and Studies, c. N. Tasoudi (third book), Athens, 1977.]
ΒιογραφικαὶἈναμνήσεις τοῦἈρχιεπισκόπου Ἀθηνῶν Χρυσάνθου τοῦἀπὸ Τραπεζούντος (1881-1949), Ἀθῆναι, 1970. [ViografikaiAnamniseis touArchiepiskopou Athena Chrisanthou touapo Trapezountos (1881-1949), Athens, 1970.]
Ἔργον τῶν Ἀποστόλων τοῦὙπουργείου Περιθάλψεως» (Πόντος, Κωνσταντινούπολις, Σμύρνη, Μακεδονία), Ἐν Ἀθήναις 1920. [Work of mission touYpourgeiou Welfare "(Sea, Constantinople, Smyrna, Macedonia), in Athens 1920]
Ζηζιούλας Ιω. Δ., Ἰερουσαλήμ, ἘκκλησιαστικὴἸστορία, Θρησκευτικὴ καὶἨθικὴἘγκυκλοπαίδεια, τ. 6ος, Ἀθῆναι, 1965, 839-843. [Zizioulas Io. D., Jerusalem, EkklisiastikiIstoria, religious kaiIthikiEgkyklopaideia T. 6th, Athens, 1965, 839-843.]
Κονιδάρης Γερ. Ι., Ἀντιόχεια, Θρησκευτικὴ καὶἨθικὴἘγκυκλοπαίδεια, τ. 2ος, Ἀθῆναι, 1963, 878-908. [Konidaris Ger. I., Antioch, religious kaiIthikiEgkyklopaideia, vol. 2nd, Athens, 1963, 878-908.]

In: Religion and Public Life
Editor: David Muskhelishvili

ISBN: 978-1-53618-904-9
© 2021 Nova Science Publishers, Inc.

Chapter 11

THE HISTORICAL MISSION OF SVETITSHKOVELI AND GEORGIA

Manana Gabashvili[*]

Doctor of History, Leading Scientist,
Ilia University G. Tsreteli Institute of Oriental Studies, Tbilisi, Georgia

ABSTRACT

The historical mission of Svetitskhoveli is special. For centuries, it has played a major role in the religious, political, social and cultural life of the Georgian people. It is a landmark of correct values.

Keywords: Svetitskhoveli, Georgia, Mtskheta, landmark, consolidation, politics, religion, culture, endurance, hope

The historical mission of Svetitskhoveli is special. The main Georgian cathedral named as a second Jerusalem, is the symbol of unity and at the same time a great chronicle, where all the historical stages of the country's

---

[*] Corresponding Author's E-mail: mangabash@gmail.com.

life are narrated through means characteristic of art, and through inscriptions.

The presence of Christ's robe in Georgia (according to church tradition and foreign and Georgian sources) gives it particular importance and international value not only for Georgia, but for the whole Christian world, and the mission of the cathedral acquires an even greater scale.

Svetitskhoveli Cathedral is also a bearer of both ecclesiastical and secular information expressed in the frescoes and beautiful ornaments and symbols on the facade, interesting from an artistic point of view. They should be divided into two categories - carriers of hidden and open information.

Svetitskhoveli was also the place of great historical events (the coronations of kings, enthronization of Catholicoses, etc.) in all times and epochs.

The restoration of the autocephaly of the Georgian Church on March 12, 1917, the centennial of which was celebrated by Georgian people with gratitude, was also remarkable as it again preceded the political independence of Georgia. The militant nature of the Georgian Church explained with the peculiarities and complexity of the region was emphasized by it once more.

Thus, Svetitskhoveli is a cathedral of militant character that expressed itself in many periods of Georgian history. This concerns the preservation of Georgian traditions and the issue of the Georgian language as well, its care and protection, which should be considered in the common context of Svetitskhoveli and the history connected to it. Here, those heads of the cathedral who fought against the Russian Church and the expansion of Russian language after the occupation of Georgia by Russia in 1801 are implied, something akin to heroism.

At different times, fighting against Georgia meant the fighting against Svetitskhoveli as well, with weapons or ideologically, resulting in the cathedral itself and its frescoes being damaged several times. After the loss of state independence in the 19th century, some frescoes of Svetitskhoveli became victims of some conscious or unintentional actions, or of unprofessional and careless restoration. In spite of it, it is possible to restore the unbroken chain of events by means of remaining small and fragmentary material extant before the 17th century, as in the case of *The Life of Kartli*, where a continuous narrative of Georgia's ecclesiastical and secular history is given.

The scope of questions put on the frescoes of Svetitskhoveli is large and some of them have not lost their relevance even today. These are the questions of the political orientation of Georgia, marine themes, the place and role of the Georgian Church in the life of Georgia and generally in the Orthodox world, national ideology, symbolism, and so on. Thus, Svetitskhoveli is interesting because of the numerous questions (regarding domestic or foreign politics) presented within it, in which religious and secular motives are intertwined. Correspondingly, we should consider Svetitskhoveli as one of the most important sources of Georgian history. Proceeding from it, it is natural that the large amount of information contained within Svetitskhoveli and related research topics attracts a wide range of scholars. They are representatives of various disciplines - religious scholars, historians, architects, art critics, theatre experts, musicologists, astronomers, philologists, and specialists of folk and classical dancing who theoretically studied and staged dance scenes inspired by the Svetitskhoveli fresco (V. Chabukiani, L. Gvaramadze, A. Tataradze...).

Naturally, Svetitskhoveli attracts not only pilgrims from various countries, but also scholars and guests interested in the history and culture of Georgia. So, it is also greatly aids in the popularization of the history and culture of Georgia. Yet, unfortunately it has not been properly studied by Georgian historians yet.

Taking into account all the aforementioned factors, the following idea arose. We think Svetitskhoveli could be compared with *The Life of Kartli* in order to gain a fuller understanding of the cathedral and the chronicle. Their similarity is also conditioned by their location in a very complex region (at the crossroads of the East and West). Moreover, they both reflect the history of the country and the state's approach to problems, national ideology, and intransigence towards enemies. We should also consider Svetitskhoveli as an example of the political balance of a country located in the very complex region at the crossroads of the East and West. And this balance is represented in it by means inherent to art. Svetitskhoveli also manifests a coexistence with the world in terms of religion, politics and diplomacy, as evidenced by some frescoes and inscriptions made there in Georgian, Greek, and Arabic.

Another aspect bringing Svetitskhoveli closer to *The Life of Kartli* is its connection to Georgian monasteries abroad, including holy Mount Athos, which is more evidence of this cathedral's involvement in religious and secular international processes. Its relation with centers in Tao-Klarjeti, the Patriarchate of Antioch, and the Arab-speaking Orthodox world etc. is important as well [1].

It is known that most of the frescoes of Svetitskhoveli belong to the 17th century. That is why when we compare this cathedral and *The Life of Kartli*, the situation in the 17th century, as well as attitudes concerning *The Life of Kartli* and Svetitskhoveli during this period should be taken into account. The 17th century is one of the most significant eras in the life of Georgia. It is not called the Renaissance by chance. It was at this time that the importance of history and of the restoration of ties with the past was emphasized. The statesmen of those times stressed the importance of history as well as the national ideology connected to it. This had a great importance for Georgia since it was surrounded by Islamic states [2]. Education also plays a big role in such a time, which has been mentioned in many articles noting that knowledge is no less an important weapon for Georgia, without which it is difficult to conduct a proper analysis and predict events. Education is always closely connected with the situation in the country and its politics. We explain the education of the Bagrationi dynasty and the usage of education by them at various stages of Georgian history - for example, during the unification of feudal Georgia (10th century) and so on [3]. The appearance of Georgian encyclopaedists in the 17th century, in the epoch called the Small Renaissance, is not by chance either.

Starting with Sulkhan-Saba, they had been acting and creating an intellectual environment, strengthening it with practical bases, during the 17th and 18th centuries. Svetitskhoveli is included in this common atmosphere and appears as one of the popularizers of religious and secular education. It is not accidental either, that in this epoch, attention was paid to *The Life of Kartli* and work for creating *A New Life of Kartli* began in order to fill the gaps among historical events. But, besides its purely academic approach, people were familiarized with the history of Georgia with the great ideological purpose of "Life of Kartli," its circulation, and dissemination.

The Life of Kartli was the most read book in the 17th century. Everybody wished to possess this great chronicle. The role of Queen Mariam in the popularization and spread of *The Life of Kartli* is well known. It was copied out by her commission (Mariam's *The Life of Kartli*). The following fact also attracts our attention. Queen Mariam, in caring for the *The Life of Kartli*, also took care of Svetitskhoveli. The repair of the collapsed dome is connected with her name (and with the name of King Rostom). The inscriptions in the cathedral also concerning *The Life of Kartli*, are associated with her as well.

Thus, *The Life of Kartli* and Svetitskhoveli were given equal attention, confirming the idea that the Georgians of those days realized the importance of Svetitskhoveli quite well, and we also should not exclude its connection with *The Life of Kartli*. It also means understanding the history of Georgia in its entirety. Therefore we should see a direct influence of *The Life of Kartli* on some frescoes of Svetitskhoveli.

Svetitskhoveli responds to the challenges of the 17th century with its content, thus fulfilling its very important historical mission. But there are a number of topics and problems to which special attention is paid at Svetitskhoveli. In this respect, we consider the fact very significant that marine themes are represented on a large part of the south wall of Svetitskhoveli, since Kartli and this cathedral are at such a distance from the Black Sea. That has always caused astonishment and was difficult to explain. It is known that there is no other fresco like it in Georgia. We have had these questions for years. Only work on marine themes brought us to this fresco and to an attempt at comprehending it. In Georgian historiography there was a large gap concerning marine issues and work on this showed how this or that question of Georgian history is explained by marine interests and policy. These interests affected the economic situation and welfare of the West Georgian cities dependent on the situation in the Black Sea.

For example, in the 10th century, the Black Sea was closed because of the Arabian-Byzantine rivalry. This hindered the relations of the West Georgian cities with the rest of the world and especially with the West. Only in the 11th-13th centuries, when the Italians - Venetians and Genoese - entered the Black Sea and established their trading stations was the Black Sea opened up to the West and other major world centers [4].

When Svetitskhoveli frescoes were being created in the 17th century, some Ottoman aggression took place on the Black Sea and the sea even used to be called "Ottoman Lake." The Ottomans, like all other aggressors, tried to drive out Georgians from the Black Sea. The Georgians fought against this in different ways, both with weapons, and with politics and diplomacy. Periodically, they skillfully used the difficult situations in which Ottomans found themselves thus causing their serious concern. At such a time, the actualization and propagandization of the Black Sea issues had great importance, and, in our opinion, this Svetitskhoveli fresco does just that, thus it should be considered as one of the most important functions of this cathedral's mission. By means of it, the special interest and attitude of Georgians towards the sea are also emphasized. In our opinion, it has the same meaning as the sea and navigation widely represented in *The Knight in the Panther's Skin*, which has also been ignored for a long time. The fact of how deeply Shota Rustaveli knows navigation and related issues speaks volumes. It should also be taken into account that most of the navigation terms are Georgian [5]. Thus the myth about the alienation of Georgians from the sea is dissipated. It should be taken into consideration that *The Knight in the Panther's Skin,* together with *The Life of Kartli*, was one of the most read books, meaning that different generations of Georgians were in constant contact with the sea, sea themes, sea voyages, sea transport, trade, and so on, by means of it. This is also clearly seen from the rich archaeological, ethnographic, numismatic and folklore materials and myths (about the Argonauts and others).

Sea themes are also interestingly represented in *The Life of Kartli*, allowing us to shed new light on Vakhtang Gorgasali's attitude (whose portrait was destroyed in Svetitskhoveli in the 19th century during the process of restoration) regarding Trebizond in respect to Eastern and Western politics. That is, it turns out that this interest had been relevant even before Tamar's epoch [6].

The question of Trebizond was also pertinent for David Kuropalates during the process of the unification of feudal Georgia in the 10th century, but Georgian historiography has overlooked this fact. Yet the politics regarding Trebizond acquired a programmatic character just in this period, and they manifested themselves in various forms in the following epochs. The claim of inheritance by the Byzantine Empire should be connected to the same period and a similar programmatic approach finding a response in the following centuries as well [7]. Namely, long before Tamar was depicted in red shoes on the fresco in Vardzia - since only a Byzantine emperor had the right to wear them - David Kuropalates was depicted with the crown of a Byzantine emperor on a fresco in Oshki Cathedral [8].

After David, this idea is attested both in the titles of some kings (Giorgi II) and on coins (David the Builder). But these politics become the most successful during Tamar's reign. The conduct of research in this direction was hampered by the circumstance that we have already shown elsewhere. The interconnected phenomena - the foundation of the Empire of Trebizond by Tamar (1204) and the military campaign in Iran (1210) - were treated separately by Georgian historiography, so that the real scale of Tamar's politics was reduced [9]. This also applies to Tamar's marine policy, which should be divided into two stages. The foundation of the Empire of Trebizond should be implied as the first stage and the campaign against Constantinople, as seen from Georgian and Byzantine sources, as the second one [10]. Tamar began the accomplishment of this second stage through David, brother of Alexios I Komnenos (1204), whom she had established on the throne of the Empire of Trebizond. David praised Alexios and considered himself as his predecessor and herald [11]. But the appearance of the Mongols destroyed these plans. Still, this idea existed in different forms by the time the frescoes of Svetitskhoveli were created in the 17th century.

The aforementioned policy raises the question of whether this policy could be expressed in Svetitskhoveli as well. This will be discussed later. It should now be noted how much this idea was propagandized. It is seen from the works of Tamar's ode-writers that she was called "Caesar," "New Rome," "New Khosrow," and "Master of Jimshed" (Master of Persia). By this, they express her Eastern and Western politics and, what is more, the connection between her Persian politics and the foundation of the Empire of Trebizond. Shavteli also notes the fact of the foundation of the Empire of Trebizond [12]. *The Knight in the Panther's Skin*, responding to Tamar's ode-writers Shavteli and Chakhrukhadze, is also constructed according to the plot of Tamar's large-scale politics. So it is natural that Rustaveli devoted it to Queen Tamar's successful politics. Understanding the politics of Queen Tamar in such a way, it becomes clear that Gulanshasro is Trebizond and it should not be sought either in Asia, or in Europe (Venice) and, even more so, in Africa [13].

The following circumstance should also be taken into account. Since ancient times, numerous names of the Black Sea associated with Georgia and Georgians have been attested both in Georgian and foreign sources: "Sea of Colchis," "Pasiani Sea" (On the portolan of Abraham Ortelius 1590), "Sea of Lazians," "Sea of Speri," "Sea of Trebizond," "Georgian Sea," which is encountered in the work of an anonymous Persian author of the 10th century (*Hudud al-'Alam*), and to which the purely Georgian name in Georgian sources - "Sea of Speri" - corresponds (that is the same as Sea of Iberia) [14]. In a later period, "Sea of David" appears which is connected with David the Builder's name [15]. "Megrelian Sea" is the later reflection of "Sea of Colchis." The fresco in Svetitskhoveli representing marine themes corresponds to these names of the Black Sea with its artistic form. According to our observation, it obviously has the form of the Black Sea, causing an association with the Black Sea depicted on Italian portolans.

Though the fresco in Svetitskhoveli representing sea themes is in reality a reflection of Psalms 148-150, there are important secular motives on it as well and, on the whole, this fresco should be considered as one of the most interesting sources of marine history. Symbols and monsters of various types are seen in a stormy sea and Georgian flags with a golden cross on a red background are fluttering on the sailing vessels. If we decipher the language of this fresco, we will see the following historical reality. We should connect it to the situation created in the Black Sea after the fall of the Byzantine Empire (1453), the period when the Ottomans tried to become masters on the Black Sea and had the pretension of transforming it into "Ottoman Lake." As for the Georgian flag with Christian symbols, it should be understood as a symbol of Georgians fighting against Turkification and Islamization of the Black Sea [16]. This fresco is notable for another aspect as well, as it is also connected with the question of the orientation of Georgia.

It is known that in the 17th century, a process of Europeanisation was taking place in different spheres in Georgia. Some relevant studies have shown that this process affected Svetitskhoveli as well. For example, some personified symbols of the wind depicted on four corners of the fresco are characteristic only of European portolans. And the flag is analogous of the Georgian flags attested on portolans. The influence of European art is also seen on the fresco of Queen Mariam in Svetitskhoveli. In general, the Black Sea was a way for Georgia to communicate with the West. In this respect, the portolan of European Battista Agnese, 16th century, is interesting, where the gaze of a Georgian king (without the name) is directed towards the Black Sea.

While working on the fresco of Queen Mariam in Svetitskhoveli, we have seen some certain parallels with Tamar's fresco in Vardzia where by means of inscriptions, artistic methods, and symbols, the program of the Georgian state is represented - the claim of inheritance of the East and the West, Trebizond and Byzantium - from where it is seen that the foundation of the Empire of Trebizond and the campaign in Iran were seen and understood to be interrelated by the authors of the Middle Ages (the same is true for Tamar's ode-writers), unlike modern historians. For our studies, it also turned out to be very important that the fresco of Queen Mariam was characterized by the same features as the fresco in Vardzia, confirming that the former has a historical connection with the latter and represents its indirect political reflection [17]. It seems that contemporaries and among them Beri Egnatashvili did not compare Queen Mariam with King Tamar by chance [18].

Thus, in spite of the extant differences between epochs we should consider Mariam's fresco in Svetitskhoveli and Tamar's fresco in Vardzia together. Moreover, in both cases, the sea and the problems associated with it are the most important. That's why Mariam's fresco is purposefully depicted next to the fresco of the sea themes.

It is also worth of noting, that in the same epoch (16th-17th centuries), the interest towards Queen Tamar is great in eastern sources and folklore, and in the Russian legend of Dinara.

Svetitskhoveli has one more important mission. A fresco distinguished by its unusual freedom is under the fresco of marine themes, where a trio of dancing women is represented, and in the background - a round dance and a group of male musicians. In general, the Georgian dances (in this case Samaya and Perkhuli) are simultaneously a reflection of the history of Georgia and a demonstration of the Georgian character tempered in wars, a kind of propaganda of their intransigence to enemies and of their optimism [19]. It is known that Plato, Xenophon, and others viewed dances as more than just dances. Xenophon even wrote that the Chans started military actions with singing and dancing, and Ivane Javakhishvili has also noted it [20].

Platon Ioseliani (19th century) considered this feature of Georgians from a historical point of view. He noted in this regard: "Georgians combine misfortune and feast. It was so then and it is so today" [21]. We deal with the same scheme in Svetitskhoveli. The historical mission of this great cathedral is great both in this and in many other respects.

REFERENCES

[1] Chikhladze, N. *Painting of Svetitskhoveli, Collection: "Svetitskhoveli,"* 2010, p. 237.

[2] Gabashvili, V. *Vakhushti Bagrationi*, Tbilisi, 1969, pp. 28-43, 130-142.
[3] Gabashvili, M. *Education and David Kuropalates' Politics, "Logos,"* Tbilisi, 2008.
[4] Gabashvili, M. *Georgian Cities in the 9th-12th Centuries*, Tbilisi, 1981, pp. 54-63.
[5] Kutaleishvili, T. *Navigation in Georgia*, Tbilisi, 1987, p. 135.
[6] Gabashvili, M. *From the History of Vakhtang Gorgasali's Marine Policy, Academic Collection – Roin Metreveli* 70, Tbilisi, 2009.
[7] Gabashvili, M. *Preconditions of the Foundation of the Empire of Trebizond, Collection -Tamar Gamsakhurdia* 70, Tbilisi, 2007, p. 121.
[8] Jobadze, V. *Early Medieval Georgian Monasteries in Historical Klarjeti and Tao*, Tbilisi, 2006, pp. 140, 175.
[9] Gabashvili, M. *Queen Tamar's Eastern and Western Politics, Collection - Valerian Gabashvili* 90, Tbilisi, 2003, pp. 188-193.
[10] Gabashvili, M. *From the History of Queen Tamar's Marine Policy*, Collection - Valerian Gabashvili, 90, Tbilisi, 2003, pp. 165-173.
[11] Niketas Choniates, *Georgica*, VI, Tbilisi, 1966, p. 131.
[12] Gabashvili, M. King Tamar's Eastern and Western Politics According to Fiction (*The Knight in the Panther's Skin, Abdulmesiani, Tamariani*), Collection - The East and Caucasus, 3, Tbilisi, 2005, pp. 72-73; idem, Tamar's Frescoes As a Historical Source, Collection - Giorgi Nadiradze 80, Tbilisi, 2012, pp. 22-37.
[13] Gabashvili, M. *Navigation and Gulansharo's Issue in The Knight in the Panther's Skin*, Collection - Shota Meskhia 90, Tbilisi, 2006.
[14] Corresponding sources see in: M. Gabashvili, The Name "Georgian Sea" Indicating the Black Sea in Persian Historiography of the 10th century ("Hudud Al-'Alam"), Collection - Academic Paradigms, NatelaVachnadze 70, Tbilisi, 2009; idem, *The Black Sea According to Georgian Sources*, Tbilisi, Works of the State University 186, Tbilisi, 1978.
[15] Kiknadze, L. For One Name of the Black Sea, *Onomastic Collection*, Tbilisi, 1993.

[16] Gabashvili, M. Ships with Sails Showing Georgian Flags on the Fresco of Svetitskhoveli. *Scientific Journal Kartvelology*, Tbilisi, 2016, pp. 45-46, 46-77.
[17] M. Gabashvili, Fresco of Queen Mariam and Prince Otia in Svetitskhoveli Cathedral (From Historical and Artistic Point of View), *Scientific Journal Kartvelology*, Tbilisi, 6, 2017, pp. 85-94.
[18] Beri Egnatashvili, *A New Life of Kartli*, Tbilisi 11, 1959, p. 441.
[19] Gabashvili, M. Dancing Scene and Group of Musicians on the Fresco in Svetitskhoveli, *Scientific Journal Kartvelology*, 1, Tbilisi, 2017.
[20] Javakhishvili, I. *Main Issues of the History of Georgian Music*, Tbilisi, 1990, p. 211.
[21] *The Life of King Giorgi the Thirteenth, described by Platon Ioseliani*, Tbilisi, 1978, pp. 216-217.

In: Religion and Public Life
Editor: David Muskhelishvili
ISBN: 978-1-53618-904-9
© 2021 Nova Science Publishers, Inc.

Chapter 12

GEORGIAN AND FOREIGN WRITTEN SOURCES ON THE AUTOCEPHALY OF THE GEORGIAN CHURCH IN THE 5TH-12TH CENTURIES

Levan Tkeshelashvili[*], PhD
Department of Georgian History,
Gelati Theological Academy and Seminary, Kutaisi, Georgia

ABSTRACT

The Georgian Church is one of the oldest churches in the Apostolic Orthodox World. According to the old Georgian historical sources, granting autocephaly tu the Georgian church took place in the second half of the fifth century during the reign of the Georgian King Vakhtang Gorgasali. Considering the sources it can be concluded that in the second half of the fifth century there existed several bishops in Georgia mainly in large cities and religious centres. 11-th century Ephrem the Lesser (Minor) reports in one of his works that in the period of the Theophylactus of Antioch (744-750) several monks were sent from Georgia to Antioch.

---

[*] Corresponding Author's E-mail: tkeshelashvililevani564@gmail.com.

Keywords: The Georgian Church, history, sources, autocephaly, Patriarch

The ancient Church of Iberia is of apostolic origin, because five apostles of Christ preached on the territory of Georgia in the fourth decade of the first century. It was from that period that the church hierarchy arose in Georgia, which was founded directly by the apostles of Christ. Their special interest in Georgia was not accidental. It was determined by the strategic location of the Georgian state and its political "weight." This process continued in the 4th century after the announcement of the Milan Edict in 313, when in parallel with the Roman Empire, Christianity was declared as the state religion in Georgia. The coordinated and purposeful actions of the Georgian King Mirian and the Byzantine Emperor Constantine the Great (306-337) contributed to the completion of such an important undertaking. Such a close relationship between Georgia and Byzantium continued in the 5th century, when a Catholicosate was formed in the Church of Iberia. In this case, the close connection between King Vakhtang (442-502) and the Byzantine Emperor Leo the Great (457-474) is also clearly visible. According to Georgian written sources, the Georgian Church was subordinate to the most ancient Antiochian Patriarchate already in the 4th century, which was due to the geographical proximity of the Patriarchate of Antioch with Georgia.

The oldest Georgian sources *The Conversion of Kartli* and *The Life of Vakhtang Gorgasali* by Juansher connect the foundation of the Catholicosate in the Georgian Church with the conflict that took place between St. King Vakhtang Gorgasali and Archbishop Michael.

Though there are some differences between editions of *The Conversion* and Juansher's work, but the facts that the Georgian Church was subordinate to the Patriarchate of Antioch at this time and the King Vakhtang had carried out this reform thanks to his connections are obvious. According to the Georgian sources, the king returned from Persia and it was then that his confrontation with the archbishop took place. The oldest, Shatberdi version of *The Conversion of Kartli* gives us very scant information about this: "After some time he returned, and Michael was an archbishop. And he hit the king in the face with his foot" (*The Conversion* 1979:325). The source does not mention the reason for the dispute and blames the insult of the king on Michael, followed by the dispatch of representatives to Byzantium by the king, who "asked the Emperor and Patriarch to send a Catholicos to Georgia." Such scanty information causes some misunderstanding. But Juansher's work on this issue is more informative. The source tells us the reason for the confrontation and names the Byzantine Emperor, giving us the opportunity to reach certain conclusions. Juansher names Emperor Leon, who reigned until 474, so the king had sent the representatives before 474. "And Leon the Greek and his troops went to Shimshat, and Vakhtang sent an intermediary to bring him a wife, Catholicos Peter, and Bishop Samuel" (*The Life of Kartli*, 1955: 196). It is clear that by that time the first wife of King Vakhtang was supposedly dead, and the most interesting thing is the fact that during Leon the Great's reign, Vakhtang became a relative of the Emperor of Byzantium and at the same time brought the Catholicos, meaning that first the conflict between the King and Bishop had taken place, and then the king brought a wife and the Catholicos from Byzantium; thus, King Vakhtang establishes close political and religious ties with Byzantium, which was determined by his Orthodox orientation.

According to Juansher, the king had decided to bring the Catholicos from Byzantium even before the conflict, since Archbishop Michael heard about sending the delegation to Byzantium upon the king's arrival. Ekvtime Takaishvili and Sargis Kakabadze noted that the bitterness of Michael was caused by King Vakhtang requesting the government of the Empire of Eastern Rome and the Patriarch of Constantinople to appoint Peter as Catholicos. It was after this conflict that Peter was sent as Catholicos from Byzantium, and became the first Catholicos of Mtskheta.

The work *A Story on Why the Georgians Converted* by the famous Georgian public figure of the 11[th]century, Ephrem Mtsire, represents the most significant source regarding the early period of the autocephaly of the Georgian Church. The source is interesting from many points of view, including its special emphasis on the topic of the autocephaly of the Georgian Church. Ephrem's work directly proceeds from an old Greek source *The Antioch Chronicles* and is of special value. In the years of Patriarch Theophylact of Antioch (744-750), two monks who arrived from Georgia told him about their problem, since no Georgian Catholicos had been consecrated in Antioch since the time of Patriarch Anastasius (602-610) of Antioch: "No Catholicos has been consecrated for Georgians in Antioch because of difficulties in traveling" (Ephrem Mtsire, 1959: 9). This part of the work is biased, regarding which the historian B. Lominadze said: "The information that the travel of Georgians to Antioch since the time of the Patriarchate of Anastasius (602-610) was stopped due to difficulties in the journey caused by Arabs does not correspond to reality, as Arabs had captured Antioch in 633 and they appeared in Georgia in 642-643" (Lominadze, 1999:34). The information of *The Antioch Chronicles* clearly contradicts old Georgian sources, as it turns out that the Georgian Church had not had a Catholicos for 140 years, that is, from the Patriarchate of Anastasius of Antioch (602-610) up to the Patriarchate of Theophylact of Antioch (744-750), and that does not correspond to reality. About 16 Catholicoses had sat on the Patriarchal throne during this period in Mtskheta (Tkeshelashvili, 2014:94).

Despite its tendentiousness, this short paragraph from *Chronicles* confirms the fact that the Georgian Church had a Catholicos before 744-750. Perhaps the old information about the consecration of the first Catholicos of Mtskheta in Antioch during the reign of King Vakhtang, as well as subsequent Catholicoses, was reflected in *The Antioch Chronicles*. Therefore this message was erroneously extended to a later period. We must conclude that the work of Ephrem Mtsire, which originates from the foreign source, once again confirms the fact that the Georgian Church had a Catholicos until the 8th century and it indirectly indicates that the Catholicosate had existed since the period of Vakhtang Gorgasali.

The Greeks repeatedly questioned the autocephaly of the Georgian Church. St. Giorgi the Hagiorite, whose life is described by Giorgi Mtsire, made a special contribution to the protection of the rights of the Georgian Church in the 11th century. Some monks from St. Simon Lavra on the Black Mountainduring the period of Patriarch Theodosius III (1057-1076) slandered Georgians before the Patriarch of Antioch. They questioned the true faith of the Georgians: "We do not know what they think, or what their faith is"; and, according to their second accusation, allegedly, "none of the Twelve Apostles came to their country." In spite of these charges, the Greeks recognized that Georgians had an autocephalous Church by that time: "Churches and bishops of Georgians do not subordinate to any other Patriarch, and they themselves manage all church records and choose their own Catholicoses themselves" (Sabinini, 1882: 462). It is clear that Georgians were not subordinate to any other Patriarch at this time and they themselves consecrated Catholicoses. Giorgi the Hagiorite substantiated to the Greeks the legitimacy of the autocephaly of the Georgian Church by means of Greek sources. First, he made the Metropolitan, a Georgian by birth, bring *The Travels of Andrew the Apostle*, in which the reality of the activities of Andrew the First-Called in Georgia was confirmed. Giorgi the Hagiorite also told the Greeks that the second Apostle of Christ "Simon the Zealot is buried in our country, Abkhazia, which is called Nikopsi." Thanks to this, the holy Father strengthened his arguments about the activities of the Apostles in Georgia, since the fact of the burial of Simon the Zealot in Georgia was the most authentic proof of the activities of the Apostles there. This information from Giorgi the Hagiorite also proves once again that Abkhazia is the most ancient territory of Georgia. Giorgi the Hagiorite generally denied the need to link the Georgian Church with Antioch. He developed the idea that the basis of the legitimacy of autocephaly is the preaching of the Apostles in the territory of the country and that in this respect the Georgian Church enjoyed the same honor as the Antiochian Church. During argumentation he adduced the Holy Scripture as evidence, where in the first chapter of the Gospel of John it is told how Andrew brought his brother to Christ: "And he brought him to Jesus" (John 1:40-42). He showed the Greeks by this fact that the founder of the Antioch Church, Apostle Peter, was summoned by his brother Andrew, and therefore "it would be proper if he obeyed the one who called him, that is his brother Andrew." Based on the Holy Scripture, the holy Father once again showed Greeks the advantage of the Church of Iberia. At the same time he underlined the fact that the Georgian Church had been autocephalous since the first century and the preaching of the Apostles in Georgia was the basis for this.

As for the sin of heresy, Giorgi the Hagiorite, on the contrary, inculcated the Greeks in it and cited *The Great Synaxarion* to this end: "There was a time when Orthodoxy was not found in all of Greece and John, Bishop of the Goths, was consecrated as a bishop in Mtskheta, as it is written in *The Great Synaxarion.*" The Greek source *The Life of John of Gothia* proved the accusation of Giorgi the Hagiorite. The fact that the Church of Iberia was the only one in the East which had sacredly preserved Orthodoxy while the iconoclast heresy raged in the Byzantine Empire was confirmed in the life of the holy Father. That is why John of Gothia was consecrated in Mtskheta instead of Constantinople.

The information of the Patriarch of Antioch and canonist Theodore Balsamon (1186-1203) concerning the autocephaly of the Georgian Churches distinguished among foreign sources of this period. When explaining the second canon of the Second Ecumenical Council of the Christian Church held in Constantinople in 381, the Patriarch of Antioch recalls the Georgian Church. It is worth noting the fact that there are differences in the content among the translations of the Council of the Church. The version translated from Greek into Georgian and published in 1970 by S. Kaukhchishvili corresponds to the original: "Do not be surprised if you find other Churches also to be autocephalous, such as the Churches of Bulgaria, Cyprus, and Iberia... The Archbishop of Iberia was ordained according to the decree of the Council of Antioch" (Georgica VIII, 1970:18). Historian V. Goiladze paid attention to this question and remarked that there is a difference between the Greek and Latin versions of Balsamon's text (Goiladze, 1991: 140). It should be noted that the difference is so great that the content of the text is changed in the Latin translation. The Greek version: "When Peter was the Holiest Patriarch of the divine great city of Antioch, a decree was adopted by the Council stating that the Church of Iberia, which at that time was subordinate to the Patriarch of Antioch, would be free and autocephalous." The Latin version of the translation: "At the time of Peter, the Holiest Patriarch of Antioch, the Council adopted a decree stating that the Church of Iberia would be free and autocephalous but subordinate to the Patriarch of Antioch." The last paragraph in the Latin translation causes a misunderstanding. If the Council ruled that the Church of Iberia would be free and autocephalous, why did it have to stay under the authority of the Patriarch of Antioch? The Greek text is more reliable and reflects the reality. The Georgian translation of the interpretation of the Nomocanon by Nicodemus Milash corresponds to the Greek text of Balsamon: "It should not seem strange to you when we see other autocephalous churches, such as the Churches of Bulgaria, Cyprus, Iberia" (Milash I, 2007: 277). The Greek version of Balsamon's text and its Russian translation speak of the full autocephaly of the Georgian Church. It should also be noted here that the works of P. Ioseliani and Marie Brosset use the version of the Latin translation, where the content is distorted (Ioseliani, 1843: 35).

Regarding this issue, Alexander Tsagareli noted that Balsamon had stressed a fact that was already known to everyone, namely that the autocephalous Georgian Church already existed and the document confirming autocephaly could be stored in the archives of the Patriarchate of Antioch. Yet that time, Antioch was in the hands of the Crusaders, causing Balsamon to settle in Constantinople, and he did not have this document. Before becoming a Patriarch, Balsamon had been *xartophylax*, that is, the head of the Patriarchal Archive (Tsagareli, 1912:52-55).

The Church canonist and later the Patriarch of Antioch would not have mentioned the Georgian Church as autocephalous by accident when explaining the Ecumenical Councils of the Christian Church. Balsamon knew the reality exactly and that is why he mentioned the Church of Iberia among the autocephalous Churches, that is, on a par with the oldest autocephalous Churches (of Cyprus, Bulgaria, Iberia) after the autocephalous Greek Church, and recorded them into the Second Canon of the Second Ecumenical Council of the Christian Church. The information of Balsamon was reflected in a document of the Ecumenical Patriarchate from March 4, 1990, where we read: "We declare the Holy Church of Georgia with the same self-governing structure and organization which it possessed since ancient times and which is also substantiated by Balsamon who wrote: ...They say that at the time of His Holiness Peter, the Patriarch of the divine city of Antioch, the Synod adopted a decreestating that the Georgian Church would be free and autocephalous" (Japaridze 2003, III: 183). The fact that the Church of Iberia had a self-governing structure and organization since the ancient times is recognized by the decree of Patriarch Demetrios of Constantinople and the Holy Synod, and this was recorded earlier by the canonist and Patriarch of Antioch Theodore Balsamon. His information once again proved the reality that the Church of Iberia, in accordance with Church canons, is one of the oldest autocephalous churches extant in the Christian world.

REFERENCES

[1] Georgica VIII, 1970: Georgica 1970. *The Reports of Byzantine Writers about Georgia*, Texts with Georgian translation with references are published by Simon Kaukhchishvili, Tbilisi.
[2] Goiladze, V. *Regarding the Origins of the Georgian Church*, Tbilisi 1991.
[3] John: *The New Testament of Our Lord and Jesus Christ*, 2005, Tbilisi.
[4] Lominadze, B. *The Administrative Organization of the Georgian Orthodox Church in the 5th century. Collection: Issues of History of Feudal Epoch Georgia*, VII, Tbilisi 1999.
[5] Milash, Nicodemus. *The Laws of the Orthodox Church with Explanations, Vol. 1.* Tbilisi 2007.
[6] Ephrem Mtsire, *A Story on Why the Georgians Converted*, Tbilisi 1959.
[7] Conversion of Kartli, 1979: Conversion of Kartli, 1979. *The Shatberdi Collection of the 10^{th}Century*, Prepared for publication by B. Gigineishvili and E. Giunashvili, Tbilisi.
[8] Sabinini, M. *The Georgian Paradise. A Full description of the Merits, Praises, and Passions of the Georgian Saints*, St. Petersburg 1882.

[9] Tkeshelashvili, L. *The Primary Questions of the History of the Autocephaly of the Georgian Church*, Kutaisi 2014.
[10] *The Life of Kartli*, 1955: Life of Kartli I, 1955. The text based on all the main manuscripts was prepared for publication by S. Kaukhchishvili, Tbilisi.
[11] Japaridze, A. *Georgian Church Councils.* Vol 3, Tbilisi 2003.
[12] Ioseliani, P. *A Short History of the Georgian Church*, St. Petersburg (in Russian), 1843.
[13] Tsagareli, A. *Articles and Notes on the Georgian Church Issue*, St. Petersburg, 1912 (in Russian).

In: Religion and Public Life
Editor: David Muskhelishvili
ISBN: 978-1-53618-904-9
© 2021 Nova Science Publishers, Inc.

Chapter 13

THE RESTORATION OF THE AUTOCEPHALY OF THE GEORGIAN CHURCH AND GEORGIAN SOCIO-POLITICAL REALITY

Otar Janelidze[*]
Gori State Teaching University, Gori, Georgia

ABSTRACT

The chapter discusses the attitude of the Georgian society and local political parties towards the restoration of the autocephaly of the Georgian Church, which was announced in Svetitskhoveli Cathedral in Mtskheta, on March 12, 1917.

Among the political organizations in Georgia, the National Democrats were distinguished by the most respect for the Orthodox Church of the country. They fully understood the moral and religious, cultural or political significance of autocephaly of Georgia, participated in the fight for autocephaly and welcomed its acquisition with admiration.

According to the party program, before the fall of the monarchy in Russia, the restoration of autocephaly was viewed with indifference by the Georgian Social Democrats (Mensheviks). Nevertheless, their leaders (Noe Jordania, Karlo Chkheidze, Irakli Tsereteli) supported the liberation

---

[*] Corresponding Author's E-mail: Otar_janelidze@yahoo.com.

of the Georgian Church from subordination to the Russian Synod. The restoration of the self-government of the Church was approved by the Georgian Socialist-Federalists, while the Georgian Bolsheviks rejected autocephaly altogether.

Georgian periodicals have widely expressed their attitude towards autocephaly. The newspaper "Georgia" appeared as its defender, while the socialist newspapers "Ertoba," "Sakhalkho Sakme," "Alioni" and others demanded secularization and religion to proclaim as matter of conscience.

A large part of the Georgian society perceived the autocephaly of the Church as a precondition for the political freedom and state independence of the country.

Keywords: Georgia, Mtskheta, church, autocephaly, Synod, political parties, periodicals, democracy, sovereignty, secularization

After the overthrow of autocracy, a provisional government announced the definition of the status of the Russian Orthodox Church as a prerogative for constituent assembly, but convening a meeting was dragged out too much. Officials in Ukraine and Georgia did not wait for the elections of the constituent assembly and made some practical steps on the way to autocephaly. Georgian bishops, together with members of the clergy and secular figures, declared the autocephaly of the Georgian Church as "being restored (continued)."

Newspapers reported this historic moment throughout Georgia. People both in East and West Georgia greeted the news on the release of the Church from captivity with pleasure and indulged in "spiritual joy and exultation."

The locum tenens of Catholicos-Patriarch of Georgia Leonide personally presented the act of the restoration of the autocephaly of the Church of Georgia to the Tbilisi Executive Committee - the actual administrative body of Georgia and of almost the entire Caucasus at that time. Soon afterwards the leader of the region, head of Ozakom V. Kharlamov arrived in Tbilisi and was introduced to the document on the restoration of autocephaly, adopted in Mtskheta on March12, by the high priest.

A little later, when the "Interparty Council," the connecting body of political forces in Georgia, was formed, the clergy decided that the autocephalous Georgian Church would act in coordination and agreement with the council.[1]

Of the political parties and currents in Georgia, the National Democrats differed in their profound respect for the Orthodox Church of Georgia. They especially noted the historical contribution of the Church in strengthening the national idea, unity of Georgians, and integrity of the state. They substantiated the canonical, moral, religious, cultural, civil, and political importance of autocephaly. The National Democrats perceived the liberation from the prolonged domination of the Synod as "the second birth" of the Church, an achievement of spiritual freedom, and as a courageous step towards the state independence of Georgia, and welcomed it sincerely. They supported the Church and cared for its renewal and strengthening in word and deed. They carried out the popularization of autocephaly in broad masses, as evidenced by the public lectures of Sergi Gorgadze. The locum tenens of Catholicos-Patriarch of Georgia Leonide, Bishop Anton, and many other representatives of the clergy attended one of these lectures on March 28, 1917.[2]

It is worth of noting that leaders of the National Democrats appealed to the Georgian clergy to rise above the obedience and idleness set by the Synod, reject bureaucracy in the Church, make education, generosity, and self-sacrifice for the Church their vocation, and adjust their functions to the requirements of modern life.[3]

The Georgian Social-Federalists also supported autocephaly, though their party shared the idea of secularization. They demanded separation of the Church from the state and transformation religion into a free affair of believers. "Every believer should rejoice the day when the state and the Church would be separated, when the fragile Church would be free of the rough influence of the state and "the things that are Caesar's" would get

---

[1] O. Janelidze, Essays from the History of the National Democratic Party of Georgia, Tbilisi, 2002, p. 289.
[2] Newspaper "Sakartvelo," March 31, 1917.
[3] Newspaper "Sakartvelo," September 21, 1917.

detached from "the things that are God's"[4], but until that happens and the Church of Georgia fights against oppression from the Synod, "it should find a supporter in every socialist and revolutionist," - they thought.[5]

The position of the Social-Democrats (Mensheviks) was different. They, as atheists, paid less attention to religion. They indifferently looked at the restoration of the autocephaly of the Church of Georgia before the overthrow of the monarchy in Russia. This issue did not become a priority for them even after the February revolution, though several prominent leaders of the party supported the idea of the liberation of the Church of Georgia from the Church of Russia. It is known that Karlo Chkheidze and Irakli Tsereteli put in a good word for the restoration of autocephaly before the provisional government.

And according to memories of a well-known religious figure, Archpriest Nikita Talakvadze, Noe Jordania, a leader of the Tbilisi Council of Worker's Deputies and a representative of the Tbilisi Executive Committee, as well as prominent social democrat Alexandre Lomtatidze took part in the work of a special meeting held in Archpriest Talakvadze's flat on March 8, 1917, which was devoted to the consideration of the practical issues of the announcement of autocephaly. At the meeting Jordania gave "political directives" to the members of the meeting, and on March 12 it was exactly Alexandre Lomtatidze who made the first speech and welcomed the announcement of autocephaly in the yard of Svetitskhoveli Cathedral in Mtskheta[6].

How did periodicals respond to this event of great importance in the life of the nation? It can be said without exaggeration, that there was not a single Georgian journal or newspaper, which did not express its attitude to the aforementioned news.

The provisional government of the Church received letters and telegrams with greetings and congratulations and expressions of delight of clergymen, public figures, and common people from different regions, villages, cities, and institutions of Georgia. Such material was mainly

---

[4] Newspaper "Sakhalkho Sakme," August 29, 1917.
[5] Newspaper "Sakhalkho Sakme," October 12, 1917.
[6] N. Talakvadze, From the Diary of Citizen-Priest, Tbilisi, 2013, p. 97.

published in the National Democratic newspaper "Sakartvelo." The Federalist "People's Affair" widely covered the issue of the announcement of autocephaly and subsequent peripetia concerning the Church of Georgia, but this edition, like the newspaper of the Social Democrats, "Alioni," insisted on secularization - the separation of the Church from the state and the declaration of faith as a matter of conscience.

We should also add that "People's Affair" boldly stood up for the Church of Georgia when the new government of Russia recognized only its national character, did not recognize its autocephaly on a territorial basis, and established the Caucasian exarchate for the non-Georgian Orthodox community (Russians, Abkhazians, Greeks, and others) headed by the Russian metropolitan.[7] This fact was considered by the newspaper as "despotic arbitrariness" of the provisional government, an infringement of the rights of the Georgian nation, and trampling on the feelings and thoughts of its believers.[8]

In Social Democrat press the establishment of autocephaly was considered as "a split and treason of the whole revolutionary democracy." In the opinion of the newspaper "Ertoba," the Church expressed the interests only of those clerical circles and nationalistic groups which "wear the clothes of democratism and actually serve the reactionary cause."[9] The Georgian people will not agree if the clergy appropriates their property. "The Georgian people will not stand priests' domination... No subsidy to the Church from the treasury, no kopeck in favor of Church servants! The provision of the clergy or any other material support should be announced as an affair of believers itself"[10], such was a conclusion of the newspaper.

In a Social Democrat paper with comic bias "Eshmakis Matrakhi" ("Devil's Whip") a play "Autocephaly" was published. The work

---

[7] Сборник указов и постановлений Временного правительства, вып. 1, Петроград, 1917, с. 305-306. http://elib.shpl.ru/ru/nodes/10721-vyp-1-27-fevralya-5-maya-1917-1917#page/1/mode/grid/zoom/4 Вестник Временного правительства, 1917, № 140. http://elib.shpl.ru/ru/nodes/31247-140-26-avg#page/1/mode/grid/zoom/8.
[8] Newspaper "Sakhalkho Sakme," October 17, 1917.
[9] Newspaper "Ertoba," September 20, 1917.
[10] Newspaper "Ertoba," March 30, 1917.

represented a certain caricature of the clergy expecting only personal welfare from the restoration of the autocephaly of the Church.[11]

It seems that there really should have been priests with such views in Georgia at that time. The report of Archpriest Nikita Talakvadze provides a possibility of saying it, according to which the clergy had appeared "poisoned by the atmosphere of slavery and decay for 100 years."[12]

The aforementioned play exposed and mocked precisely such representatives of the clergy. Unlike the journal, Georgian Bolsheviks generally denied autocephaly and Philipe Makharadze considered a church "to obscure the very concept of democracy."[13]

The attitude of Georgian political parties towards the Church was impressively manifested at a meeting of the Tbilisi Council of Workers' Deputies. According to a statement by Social Democrat (Menshevik) Razhden Arsenidze, "Autocephaly is gaining the character of a national renaissance, the influence of the Church establishes ignorance and the domination of undesirable elements in society." The draft resolution introduced by him states: "The Council struggles fiercely with the organization of Catholicosate as a national political institution."[14] The National Democrats condemned such a position. Giorgi Gvazava called the resolution tactless, and Grigol Veshapeli took it as an insult to the feelings of the Georgian nation.[15]

Speaking on behalf of the Bolsheviks, Philipe Makharadzeannounced: "We cannot welcome the restoration of autocephaly, moreover, it is not an issue of importance, something worthy of discussion in the city council." The Socialistrevolutionaries demanded to remove this question from the agenda so as not to cast a shadow on the Church, which had just restored autocephaly. As a representative of the Armenian Democratic party, Arutinov saw it, the restoration of the autocephaly of the Church of Georgia "is a great state and revolutionary act."

---

[11] Journal "Eshmakis Matrakhi," #20, May 14, 1917, pp.6-7.
[12] N. Talakvadze, From the Diary of Citizen-Priest, Tbilisi, 2013, p. 151.
[13] Newspaper "Alioni," September 3, 1917.
[14] Newspaper "Sakhalkho Saqme," March 21, 1917.
[15] Newspaper "Ertoba," September 20, 1917, Newspaper "Sakartvelo," September 20, 1917.

We are obliged to congratulate the Georgian people, their Catholicos-Patriarch, and not treat the content. In the view of the Armenian Dashnaks, Georgian believers gathered at their discretion and a fact of a violation of freedom of conscience in their action is not observed.[16]

The Council determined by a majority vote to return to this issue at the next meeting, however the relevant protocols do not show that this issue became the subject of discussion of this body again.[17] And according to a newspaper, at the next meeting this issue was removed from the agenda per the proposal of Noe Jordania, as it "does not refer to the Council." The majority of the Council also rejected Grigol Veshapeli's suggestion to greet the autocephalous Church of Georgia.[18]

The declarative speech of the Georgian Social Democrats was of a pure political nature and was unnecessary in such an institution as the Tbilisi municipal government. Raphiel Ingilo wrote about this. According to him, the "political act" of the Mensheviks on September 18 served as just another advertisement of their party program and had no value from a political point of view.[19]

The progressive Georgian clergy imagined the mission of the autocephalous Church of Georgia in the following way: "to serve your native nation, its moral education and development, refinement, and the acquisition of self-awareness and national success."[20]

The restoration of autocephaly was important not only for the Church, but it also had a great public significance: the spiritual liberation of the nation became a harbinger for the political freedom and state independence of the country. As the famous publicist of the Federalists Samson Dadiani wrote, autocephaly is an act of historical importance. It is a step on the way to the liberation of Georgia, it accustoms the Georgian nation to the fight for its own political rights.[21] And indeed, the restoration of the autocephaly

---

[16] Newspaper "SakhalkhoSakme," March 21, 1917.
[17] Протоколы закавказских революционных советских организаций, т. 1, Тифлис, 1920.
[18] Newspaper "Sakhalkho Sakme," October 12, 1917.
[19] Newspaper "Sakartvelo," September 21, 1917.
[20] Newspaper "Sakartvelo," March 21, 1917.
[21] Newspaper "Sakhalkho Sakme," September 10, 1917.

of the Church was followed by the restoration of the independence of the Georgian state on May 26, 1918.

A very complicated 73 years will pass from this day and released from the shackles of Soviet ideology, the Church of Georgia will acquire international recognition of its autocephaly due to the great efforts of Catholicos-Patriarch, His Holiness Ilia II. This fact also preceded the day of the declaration of the restoration of Georgia's independence, April 9, 1991. The Church of Georgia illuminated the road for the newly restored Georgian state and stood in the service of spiritual development of its nation once more.

REFERENCES

Monographs

Janelidze, Otar, *Essays from the History of the National Democratic Party of Georgia*, Tbilisi, 2002.
Talakvadze, Nicita, *From the Diary of Citizen-Priest*, Tbilisi, 2013.
Протоколы закавказских революционных советских организаций, т. 1, Тифлис, 1920. [*Protocols of the Transcaucasian revolutionary Soviet organizations, vol. 1,* Tiflis, 1920.]

Periodical Press

Journal "Eshmakis Matrakhi," #20, May 14, 1917.
Newspaper "Alioni," September 3, 1917.
Newspaper "Ertoba," March 30, 1917.
Newspaper "Ertoba," September 20, 1917.
Newspaper "Sakhalkho Saqme," March 21, 1917.
Newspaper "Sakhalkho Sakme," August 29, 1917.
Newspaper "Sakhalkho Sakme," September 10, 1917.
Newspaper "Sakhalkho Sakme," October 12, 1917.

Newspaper "Sakhalkho Sakme," October 17, 1917.
Newspaper "Sakartvelo," March 21, 1917.
Newspaper "Sakartvelo," March 31, 1917.
Newspaper "Sakartvelo," September 20, 1917.
Newspaper "Sakartvelo," September 21, 1917.

Electronic Sources

Вестник Временного правительства, 1917, № 140. http://elib.shpl.ru/ru/nodes/31247-140-26-avg#page/1/mode/grid/zoom/8. [Bulletin of the Provisional Government, 1917, No. 140.]

Сборник указов и постановлений Временного правительства, вып. 1, Петроград, 1917, с. 305-306. http://elib.shpl.ru/ru/nodes/10721-vyp-1-27-fevralya-5-maya-1917-1917#page/1/mode/grid/zoom/4.
[Collection of decrees and resolutions of the Provisional Government, vol. 1, Petrograd, 1917, p. 305-306]

In: Religion and Public Life
Editor: David Muskhelishvili

ISBN: 978-1-53618-904-9
© 2021 Nova Science Publishers, Inc.

Chapter 14

THE MISSIONARY WORK OF CATHOLICOS-PATRIARCH OF ALL GEORGIA, THE ARCHBISHOP OF MTSKHETA-TBILISI AND METROPOLITAN BISHOP OF BICHVINTA AND TSKHUM-ABKHAZIA, HIS HOLINESS AND BEATITUDE ILIA II DURING THE 40 YEARS OF HIS PATRIARCHATE

Metropolitan Nicholas (Pachuashvili)[*]
of Akhalkalaki and Kumurdo

ABSTRACT

The chapter describes in detail the missionary work of the Catholicos-Patriarch of All Georgia, Archbishop of Mtskheta-Tbilisi and Metropolitan of Bichvinta and Tskhum-Abkhazia, His Holiness and Beatitude Ilia II during the 40 years of the Patriarchate.

---

[*] Corresponding Author's E-mail: m.nicholas@mail.ru.

The past period for Georgia, as for other former Soviet republics, was an era of very complex historical changes and still remains so. The collapse of the atheistic empire struggling against God caused society to irreversibly strive for freedom from slavery and to move from godlessness to faith. At that time the Lord appointed the helmsman for all Georgia who has since been consistently leading believers to the Promised Land and he, a single man, changed all of Georgia - and not only Georgia - together with the Holy Synod and clergymen consecrated by him.

Keywords: missionary work, merit, the Catholicos-Patriarch of All Georgia, Ilia II

On December 25, 2017 the Georgian Orthodox Church celebrated the 40th anniversary of the enthronement of His Holiness and Beatitude, Ilia II, Catholicos-Patriarch of All Georgia, Archbishop of Mtskheta-Tbilisi, and Metropolitan Bishop of Bichvinta and Tskhum-Abkhazia.

This past period for Georgia, as for other former Soviet republics, was an era of very complex historical changes and still remains so. The collapse of the atheistic empire struggling against God caused society to irreversibly strive for freedom from slavery and to move from godlessness to faith. At that time the Lord appointed the helmsman for all Georgia who has since been consistently leading believers to the Promised Land.

There were naturally a lot of obstacles, weaknesses, and mistakes on this very complicated journey, but today, after looking back on these 40 years, this missionary endeavor accomplished by Catholicos-Patriarch Ilia II to bring the Georgian people to God causes astonishment and admiration. It is impossible to fully describe this merit. We can only give an incomplete list of the main deeds.

How did His Holiness and Beatitude Ilia II manage to transform society so radically and form a large flock after centuries of trials and 70 years of communist regime's struggle against God?

He has been preaching all his conscious life and has been preaching everywhere: at school, the theological seminary and academy, and while being a priest and bishop, but his preaching has acquired special significance since the first day of his patriarchate. There were rumors that the new Patriarch was speaking in a language understandable to ordinary people, and this was an impressive novelty.

Church services became frequent. The parish became motivated to come to church more often. In addition to Saturdays, Sundays, and holidays, the Catholicos-Patriarch also blessed the children every Monday during the prayer service at Sioni Cathedral. On Tuesdays, after a small prayer, three clergymen preached, often including His Holiness and Beatitude Ilia II himself. A reading room was arranged in a small chapel at the church. Some courses for Psalm readers and chanters were created. Groups of Psalm readers were also formed.

In the yard where the patriarchal residence was situated, Tbilisi Sioni Cathedral became the centre of the national movement and the first Georgian sacristans were the initiators and future leaders of this movement. They often met the Catholicos-Patriarch, and this played a great role in the complicated process of the unification of Georgia.

The priesthood was limited and nearly banned during the Soviet epoch. Catholicos-Patriarch Ilia II himself embarked on the implementation of this very difficult task - choosing clergymen from a spiritually weakened nation, conducting their ordinations, and bringing them up.

Obviously, such a quick increase in the number of clergymen in a society estranged from religion and church life, in conditions when these clergymen had not receive any spiritual education since childhood, is fraught with mistakes and weaknesses and, from the very beginning, the Catholicos-Patriarch took full responsibility. His special tolerance was conditioned by it. He still tries to not punish anyone, but to take the burden on himself and correct the mistakes of others by praying. And punishment, if it is necessary, is God's will.

In 1987, icons began to be hosted by families, and this continues to this day.

In the middle of the week a parish day was established, when a priest and members of his parish used to gather and do useful work for society. Besides, parishes were commissioned to find socially unprotected people - by that time their number was small - and visit them systematically.

Subsequently, the creation of special homes for homeless children was added to this. Such activities were unimaginable before, as in accordance with Soviet law, the Church was forbidden to do charity.

Catholicos-Patriarch Ilia II especially cared about parents with deceased children, whose number increased considerably in the 1990s. His personal sympathy gave many of them the will to live. Every Saturday a special church service dedicated to the memory of the deceased children was held in at Sioni Cathedral, and later, in 1994, with the support of such parents, a free cafeteria was opened at the Patriarchate. It fed about a hundred people every day and saved thousands of lives. It still functions. Today, the International Charity Fund of the Catholicos-Patriarch of All Georgia, the "Lazare" Charity Fund of the Patriarchate, children's houses, shelters for the elderly, and other charitable organizations are active in the Church.

In 1978, a coloured, illustrated journal "Jvari Vazisa" ("Cross of Vines") was published which was first printed biannually; morning, noon day, and Eucharist prayers were published, which became a bibliographic rarity immediately. In 1979-88, prayers, Psalms, separate chapters from the Old and New Testaments, the Great Nomocanon, the Epistles of Saint Ignatius the God-bearer, and other theological texts were published in church calendars. In 1978, the periodical edition "Theological Collection" was founded, in which theological, philosophical, and historical studies and translations were published.

A complete text of the Bible in Georgian was extant only in manuscripts, in the Old Georgian language. In the 19th century, the Bible was published, but its text was incomplete and difficult to understand for readers. Moreover, practically nobody had this book. With the blessing of the Catholicos-Patriarch, an academically established text of the Bible was put together and as a result of many years of work the complete text of the Bible was first published in the modern Georgian language in 1989.

In 1988, for the first time after 800 years, the highest institute of theological study - Tbilisi Theological Academy was opened in Georgia which was followed by the foundation of other higher theological and civil educational institutions throughout Georgia.

The newspaper "Madli" ("Grace") was issued in 1989, and "Sapatriarkos Utskebani" ("Proceedings of the Patriarchate") - in 1999. Numerous different religious journals, newspapers, and web-sites are available today.

In 1988, His Holiness and Beatitude Ilia II traveled to Javakheti, which during the Soviet period was considered a closed border region and only its population was allowed to be there. The Catholicos-Patriarch discharged himself from the list of residents in Tbilisi and got registered in the Javakhetian village of Poka as a permanent resident where the Poka Saint Nino Convent has been in operation since 1992. In 1989, the Poka Saint Nino Convent was founded and a refectory was built under the open air beside the lake, where for nearly 30 years, a solemn church service has been held on June 1, the day St. Nino came to Georgia. Here, a prayer procession of believers starts on Saint Nino's route - from Lake Paravani to Mtskheta.

In 1991, the Department of Missions and Evangelism was founded at the Patriarchate, giving a greater scope to the missionary activities of the Catholicos-Patriarch.

At various times prayer processions took place in Georgian dioceses, and in 2000 and 2005, these groups went around on foot along the routes of Saint Nino and Saint Andrew the First Called to all the regions of Georgia; in 2006-2007, an exact copy of the icon of the Most Holy Theotokos of Iveron arrived from Athos and travelled all over Georgia. Now exact copies of the icons of the Most Holy Theotokos of Iveron and of the Most Holy Theotokos of Atskuri are travelling in Georgia. During these travels thousands of people were baptized and received communion, numerous young or adult couples got married in church, and houses, villages, and cities were blessed.

Since 2001, summer student expeditions have been held in Javakheti, in which students of secular higher educational institutes take part. Many new Christian families have been formed among the participants of these expeditions.

In 2002, His Holiness and Beatitude founded the International Centre of Christian Studies, which has organized 5 international symposiums, academic conferences and seminars, educational lectures, 5 academic expeditions; the Centre publishes the journal "Logos" and other literature.

Iveria Radio of the Georgian Patriarchate has been broadcasting since 2002, and since 2008 - the television station of the Georgian Patriarchate "Ertsulovneba" ("Unanimity").

Church heraldry was created and developed. His Holiness and Beatitude Ilia II is the author of the flag of the Georgian Church, on which the cross of Saint Nino is depicted, as well as of the five-cross flag of state, which beforehad been a church flag for many years. The Catholicos-Patriarch also created a coat of arms for the Patriarchate.

His Holiness and Beatitude Ilia II personally visited penitentiary institutions, including prisoners sentenced to death. In 1997, the Parliament of Georgia, at the Patriarch's proposal, passed a law abolishing capital punishment, as well as one prohibiting euthanasia and participation in it.

A law prohibiting euthanasia, which saved lives of numerous people, is in force only in some countries, including Georgia.

In 2002, a constitutional agreement between the Georgian state and the Autocephalous Georgian Apostolic Church was signed after a lengthy joint session, by which historical justice was restored and the place of the Church in the life of our country was defined. Other agreements were also signed between the Church and the state, in particular, with the Ministries of Justice, Education and Sciences, Economic Development, and Defense.

The 2,000th anniversary of Christmas was celebrated in Georgia especially solemnly.

On December 25, 1999, on the day of his enthronization - Ilia II, on behalf of the Georgian people, read a confession of sins committed over the course of these 2,000 years, especially during the 20th century, and forgave the sins of the entire nation.

On January 7, 2000, at Christmas, he was with a large delegation at a jubilee church service in Jerusalem, Bethlehem, where all Orthodox Patriarchs and Presidents had gathered.

The prayer procession "Alilo" was restored in Georgia, which has been held on a large scale basis since 2000.

On January 7, 2000, a solemn service was held at the height of 4100 meters in Betlemi Cave on Mkinvari Mountain with the help of some mountain climbers. Earlier, in 1998, by the blessing of His Holiness and Beatitude, the Holy Trinity Church made of aluminium was erected on the slope of Mkinvartsveri at the height of 4000 meters. The church is functional up to this day.

After many centuries, the rite of canonization was restored in Georgia, without which an autocephalous church cannot function.

The strengthening of the Church was followed by extensive construction activities. In 1988, His Holiness and Beatitude Ilia II created the Architectural Council of Scientific Consultation for the restoration of traditional architecture and the installation of new art forms corresponding to it. In 2003, the Georgian Patriarchate Centre of Architecture, Art, and Restoration was founded on the basis of this council. It creates, considers, and approves architectural and fine art projects and protects cultural heritage together with corresponding structures of the state. Many churches and monasteries were built, renewed, and restored.

For the first time in the history of Georgia, some dioceses of the Georgian Orthodox Church were founded abroad.

Besides, some Georgian centers named after the Holy Prophets Elijah and Enoch were opened in Jerusalem and another center dedicated to Saint George - in Lod.

Georgian monks labor on Mount Athos in different monasteries.

His Holiness and Beatitude attached special importance to the development of science and art. He is an Honorary Member of the Georgian National Academy of Sciences, an Honorary Doctor and a Professor of Ivane Javakhishvili Tbilisi State University, as well as a Doctor of Theology of many theological academies. By his blessing, in 1995, Gelati Academy of Sciences was restored. Hundreds of young people master various professions in educational institutions of the Georgian Orthodox Church. The tradition of "Thursdays" was restored, founded by Saint Catholicos-Patriarch Kalistrate Tsintsadze.

At the beginning of 1980s, the churches of Didube and Sioni were painted by the blessing of His Holiness and Beatitude Ilia II, laying a foundation for the restoration of Georgian icon painting. The icon of Saint Queen Tamar on the wall of Didube Church was created by the Patriarch himself. He is an author of many other icons.

The ancient Georgian tradition of cloisonne enamel has also been restored and developed since 1980s by his blessing. Afterwards, the Fokani Workshop was formed, which is now famous all over the world.

Calligraphy was also developed. A unique New Testament of a large size was copied by hand and decorated with miniatures and is kept at the Holy Trinity Patriarchal Cathedral.

Some embossing, icon tapestry weaving, and felt art workshops were organized; Georgian church embroidery was developed.

Forgotten Georgian chanting was also restored. 40 years ago European and Russian chants were performed in Georgian churches. From the very first days of his patriarchate, His Holiness and Beatitude Ilia II ordered Georgian composers to write liturgical and other chants, and later, through the initiative of Anchiskhati chanters, ancient Georgian chant was restored, which today is practically performed in all Georgian churches.

The Catholicos-Patriarch himself has composed some eternal chants.

Church economic activity was restored and developed by the assistance of the Catholicos-Patriarch. Sericulture was restored and developed. Georgian varieties of wheat were spread. The tradition of wine making and old wine cellars was restored in dioceses and monasteries. Great attention is also paid to the planting of greenery.

His Holiness and Beatitude Ilia II especially prays and cares for the Georgians living abroad. In 1992, the World Congress of all Georgians was held for the first time by his blessing, which was repeated several times and became the basis for the return of many people torn away from homeland. The warm and friendly relations of the Georgian Orthodox Church with Georgian Jews living in Israel should be especially noted, which is a unique example of tolerance.

Catholicos-Patriarch Ilia II enjoys great authority in Georgia: sociological studies confirm that for many years the absolute majority of the Georgian population trusts him most of all.

He is known and respected all over the world. Throughout his 40-year patriarchate, he has personally met many prominent and influential persons of the world.

The Catholicos-Patriarch reacts to every important event and examines it from a Christian point of view due to which he is involved in the processes taking place in Georgia and all over the world.

At the beginning of the 20thcentury, before the restoration of the autocephaly of the Georgian Orthodox Church, there were only five dioceses in the Georgian exarchate subordinated to the Russian Church. After the restoration of independence, the number of dioceses increased up to 15, but the most of them were abolished during the Soviet period.

By December25, 1977, when Ilia II became Catholicos-Patriarch of All Georgia, only 6 dioceses had bishops; only 48 churches and 2 monasteries - Samtavro and Saint Ekaterine (Olga) - were functional in the country; the Holy Scriptures, prayers, and other ecclesiastical literature were not available in Georgian, that is why believers used to copy them by hand; there were no Georgian sacristans.

But today, 40 years later, by December25, 2017, there are 49 dioceses in the Georgian Orthodox Church, seven of which, for the first time in the history, are abroad; there are 47 bishops, about 3,500 clergymen, 400 functional monasteries, and 1,500 functional churches.

Today in the Georgian Orthodox Church all bishops without exception are consecrated personally by the Catholicos-Patriarch.

A description of everything one by one is impossible. Even if it had been possible to describe what His Holiness and Beatitude has done during his 40-year patriarchate, it would have been taken the same period of time to read it, the time necessary for accomplishing these deeds, because every minute of his patriarchate was permeated with prayers and care and all these deeds are the results of his personal work and decisions.

Each new step made by His Holiness and Beatitude, every new kind deed accomplished by him, his every subsequent merit becomes more and more significant and always exceeds the sum of his previous spiritual labors. One of the clear examples of this is the canonization of Father Gabriel which happened as the result of the personal insistent demand of

138 *Metropolitan Nicholas (Pachuashvili) of Akhalkalaki and Kumurdo*

Catholicos-Patriarch, His Holiness and Beatitude Ilia II and the unanimous agreement of the members of the Holy Synod. His Holiness and Beatitude saw Father Gabriel's personality when he was persecuted, tortured, and insulted by men, he sheltered him, cleaned him like a pearl fallen into the dirt, and showed his magnificence to the whole world.

And if today a man exists on earth, about whom it could be boldly said that he, a single man, changed all of Georgia - and not only Georgia - during the past 40 years, this is Catholicos-Patriarch of all Georgia, the Archbishop of Mtskheta-Tbilisi and Metropolitan Bishop of Bichvinta and Tskhum-Abkhazia, His Holiness and Beatitude Ilia II together with the Holy Synod and clergymen consecrated by him, Amen!

In: Religion and Public Life
Editor: David Muskhelishvili
ISBN: 978-1-53618-904-9
© 2021 Nova Science Publishers, Inc.

Chapter 15

THEOLOGICAL EDUCATION IN GEORGIA DURING THE INCUMBENCY OF HIS HOLINESS AND BEATITUDE ILIA II, CATHOLICOS-PATRIARCH OF ALL GEORGIA

Protopresbyter Giorgi Zviadadze[*]
Doctor of Theological Sciences, Professor,
Rector of Tbilisi Theological Academy and Seminary,
Tbilisi, Georgia

ABSTRACT

The chapter discusses the importance of theological education and its history, starting from the first and the second centuries to the later epoch. A special attention is paid to the most important Georgian educational centers based in Georgia and abroad, such as monasteries of South Georgia, those on Mount Sinai and Mount Athos, Gelati Academy, the Petritsoni Monastery and others. A special research has been done on how all this was reflected in the highly fruitful ecclesiastical and educational activity of His Holiness Ilia II which he carried out throughout many years.

---

[*] Corresponding Author's E-mail: giorgi@globalmail.ge.

Keywords: Patriarch, theology, education, church, salvation, apostolic, school, monastery, academy, polycephalon

The history of educational work in Georgia begins in the ancient past. Despite the fact that the majority of sources depicting the mentioned activity have not survived to this day, on the basis of those monuments that have, it can be conclusively stated that:

The God-pleasing work of the enlightenment of the people was at all times conducted by the Apostolic Church of Georgia, whose infallible vision encompassed every corner of the land, calling into her bosom the entire nation to lead them towards salvation.

According to the history of the Church, the first theological schools were established in the 2nd and 3rd centuries. These schools were, on the one hand, the Alexandrian School of Catechesis, founded by Saint Athenagoras of Athens and Pantenos of Alexandria at the end of the 2nd century, and on the other hand, the School of Antioch, established by Saint Lucian of Antioch in the 270s. Some scholars attribute the establishment of the latter to Theophilus of Antioch, a holy Father who lived and worked in the second half of the 2nd century, while others shift the initiation of the aforementioned school to the second half of the 4th century, naming Diodorus of Tarsus and Theodorus of Mopsuest as its founders.

As well as these schools, there existed the most significant theological centers in Jerusalem, Rome, Carthage, then in Constantinople, Cappadocia, etc. In the first half of the 4th century, along with these schools, monasteries and abodes in the wilderness and, at times, even the cells of hermits appeared as complete schools in their own right.

As for Georgia, it is clear that the foundations for the work of enlightenment in the bosom of the Church were initially laid in the town of Mtskheta, and shortly after (almost immediately) they expanded throughout the land and rapidly spread beyond it.

According to surviving sources, in this respect, the most prominent of the country's regions was South Georgia until the 10th century, while beyond its borders, the Lavra of Sabatsminda was the most well-known.

These two hotbeds of education were spiritually bound together, although they were far away from each other.

The result of their cooperation is the existence of numerous liturgical manuscripts and those of other various contents. To mention one: the outstanding homiletical collection "The Sinai Polycephalon," written in 864. This is the earliest dated Georgian manuscript. It has been indisputably proved that the work was rewritten by Monk Makarius Leteleli who was sent to the Lavra of Sabatsminda from South Georgia. He is also known as the disciple of Grigol of Khandzta.

Among the Georgian monasteries functioning outside of Georgia, the Lavra of Sabatsminda was truly in the vanguard of the enlightenment until the mid-10th century, when due to extremely tough conditions, almost the entire community of Georgian monks moved to Mount Athos which allowed them to continue their work. Among them was the illustrious Georgian liturgist Ioane-Zosime, who started his unremitting activity at Sabatsminda and further continued his work of rewriting, compiling, and providing commentaries on manuscripts on Mount Sinai.

At that time, the Church Fathers of South Georgia, along with those of Sabatsminda and Sinai, embraced God-pleasing activity on Mount Athos. Among them was Ioane (John) the Athonite who formerly had worked, precisely, in South Georgia. This Holy Father is truly worthy of all reverence for he is the person who raised and educated his remarkable son Euthymius the Athonite, an outstanding theologian, who later became the luminary of the church of Georgia. Saint Euthymius the Athonite died in 1028. Ioane (John) the Athonite, the Father of Saint Euthymius, was uniquely remarkable himself as shown by an unprecedented display of regard when Saint Athanasius the Great dedicated a special "Kharisterion," a "letter of gratitude" to him, personally, and to the entire Georgian nation, whose representative he was. The original text published in Greek, meets the highest level of scholarly requirements. In recent years, a Georgian translation of the aforementioned text has been carried out and published.

A tangible attestation of the spiritual inseparability of South Georgia and Mount Athos is the well-known Bible of Oshki which was rewritten in Oshki, in South Georgia, for the Georgian brotherhood of the Monastery of

Iveron. The spiritual aspect of this relation attesting the same attachment is the fact that in the first half of the 9th century, Hieromonk Giorgi-Prokhore of Shavsheti commences with the construction of one of the greatest theological centers, the Monastery of the Holy Cross in Jerusalem with the blessing of Euthymius the Athonite himself.

It is a significant fact that Saint Giorgi the Athonite, who further promoted and honoured Euthymius the Athonite's heritage, was also educated in South Georgia. He later continued a monk's God-pleasing labor in Antioch, accomplishing his life with godly ascetics on Mount Athos as the great theologian and translator on a par with Euthymius.

On the Black Mountain, Saint Eprem Mtsire, undertook the oversight of the work of translating Greek writings into Georgian, initiated by Saint Giorgi the Athonite, enriching the Georgian Church with translations of writings, inscriptions and wills, all of paramount importance.

Saint Eprem raised Arsen, the luminary of the Church of Georgia, who apart from his abundant merit with support from King David the Builder, also undertook a special mission of establishing Gelati Theological Academy. The fruits of this endeavor have not yet been evaluated since Gelati Academy truly became a "Second Jerusalem …another Athens, yet highly surpassing it."

Apparently, the well-known theologian–Ioane Petritsi was closely connected with Gelati Academy, a prominent figure who would later bring glory and fame to the literary center of Petritsoni, another center of enlightenment of tremendous importance in the history of Georgia.

Such was that tradition, significant and solid, which during the incumbency of Patriarch Ilia II, buttressed the revival and improvement of theological enlightenment in Georgia. The yoke of atheist rule had been heaviest for the Georgian people and Georgian Church. From the very day of his enthronement, along with a crucial issue of the restoration of autocephaly to the Georgian Church, His Holiness and Beatitude Ilia II made it his aim to establish higher theological schools, which were indispensable for the attainment of another crucial goal - the revival and development of Georgian theological thought. During the period of atheist rule, Church activity was under the strict restrictions. Therefore, it is obvious that the circumstances were disadvantageous for ecclesiastical education, and therefore theological schools did not exist in the country then. Yet in 1963, a course of theological studies was initiated which in 1965 was altered into a seminary; it was, however, not a school of higher theological education in its literary meaning. With the efforts of His Holiness and Beatitude of Ilia II, Catholicos-Patriarch of All Georgia, the highest theological school – Tbilisi Theological Academy was established. Its utmost goal is to prepare scientists in the field of theology. On the very day of its inauguration, the Patriarch set an aim for this institution to unify within its walls the salvific knowledge and salvific faith: "We should not cut off ourselves from our roots, Tbilisi Theological Academy must inherit the greatest tradition of the school of theology of the highest scholarly level known as Gelati Academy. The Academy we are inaugurating today must become an important center of scholarly knowledge and spirituality" – said the Patriarch of Georgia.

In 1990, Gelati Theological Academy renewed its operations and in 1995 the Scientific Academy of Gelati was inaugurated - an event of great importance in the life of our Church and nation. The document of the inauguration was signed by President Shevardnadze, on behalf of the state, and the Catholicos-Patriarch of All Georgia, Ilia II, on behalf of the Church.

With the efforts and work of the Patriarch, theological seminaries were established in many regions of our land. For instance, the Seminary of Saint John the Theologian started to function in the town of Akhaltsikhe; the Seminary of Saint Maxim the Confessor - in the town of Tsageri; the Theological Seminary of Gremi; Saint Giorgi the Athonite High School of Church Music; College of Professional Education of Saint Euthymius the Man of God; Akhalkalaki Public College of Saint Zosime of Kumurdo and Akhalkalaki Theological School of Saint Nino. In addition, several universities for members of lay society, functioning under the aegis of the Patriarchate were established, among them are: Tbilisi Georgian University of Saint Andrew the First-Called, Tbilisi University of Saint Queen Tamar, New Georgian University of Poti,Shuakhevi University of Saint Abuserisdze of Tbeti. As well as this, parish schools were founded which function under the aegis of churches and monasteries, monastic life has been revived, the number of monasteries has increased and publishing activity has reached new heights. Numerous significant publications of the Holy Scriptures as well as of the most important theological and scientific literary works have been accomplished. All this has raised the level of the spiritual enlightenment of the people. In 2013, a Dissertation Council of Orthodox Theology was founded in Tbilisi. This event was possible due to the international authority of the Catholicos-Patriarch of All Georgia Ilia II. That same year, the Doctorate Department at Tbilisi Theological Academy started to function. Today, 23 doctoral students are studying in this department. The major subjects at this department are: Patrology, Church History, Biblical Studies, Liturgics and Canon Law. On December the 11th of 2017, the first defense of the first doctoral dissertation in theology was held. It was marked by the holy Georgian Church on a broad scale. It is natural that only a few pages cannot contain the complete description of the scale of theological and scholarly education which is directly connected with the name of His Holiness and Beatitude, Ilia II, Catholicos-Patriarch of All Georgia. Therefore, it has been our objective to give you at least a slight impression of the strenuous efforts of tremendous importance His Holiness Patriarch Ilia II has undertaken for the revival and development of the oldest traditions of the enlightenment, related to one of the most ancient Christian countries.

REFERENCES

Gamsakhurdia, Simon. *Education in Ancient Georgia*, Tbilisi, 1975.
Gangel, Kenneth O. Warren S. Benson, *Christian Education: Its History and Philosophy: Its History and Philosophy*, Wipf and Stock Publishers, 2002.
Kekelidze, K. *The Overtaking of the Georgian Literary Center by the Greeks on Mount Athos and Circumstamces in It in the 16th-17th Centuries, Episodes from the History of Old Georgian* Literature, Vol. 3, Tb. 1955, p. 69-86.

Kekelidze, K., A. Baramidze, Centers of Education and Literature in Ancient Georgia, *History of Ancient Georgian Literature* (V-XVIII centuries), Tbilisi 1969, p. 34-42.

Kiddle, Henry, Alexander Jacob Schem, *Cyclopaedia of Education: A Dictionary of Information for the Use of Teachers, School Officers, Parents and Others*, New York, 1877.

Menabde, Levan. *Centers of Old Georgian Literature*, Vol. 1, Part One, Part Two, Tb. 1962, vol. 2, Tb. 1980.

Menabde, Levan. *The Centers of Georgian Culture on Mount Athos*, Tbilisi. 1982.

Nutsubidze, Shalva. Education and Its Centers in Georgia before the VIII-X Centuries, *Critical Essays*, Tbilisi, 1965.

Seeley, Levi. *History of Education*, American Book Company, 1904.

Tavzishvili, G. *For the History of Higher Education in Georgia*, Tbilisi, 1938.

In: Religion and Public Life
Editor: David Muskhelishvili
ISBN: 978-1-53618-904-9
© 2021 Nova Science Publishers, Inc.

Chapter 16

HIS HOLINESS AND BEATITUDE CATHOLICOS-PATRIARCH OF ALL GEORGIA ILIA II AND THE MULTI-CONFESSIONAL WORLD

Sergo Vardosanidze[*]
Professor, Doctor of Historical Sciences,
Rector of Saint Andrew's Georgian University, Tbilisi, Georgia

ABSTRACT

In the chapter is shown the relation of the Georgian Orthodox Apostolic Church with the local Orthodox Churches, as well as with the leaders of different religious denominations for the last 40 years. In this context are discussed the meetings of the Catholicos-Patriarch Ilia II with the World Patriarch - Bartholomew and the leaders of the Roman Catholic Church: John-Paul II and Francis; also - interesting talks with the leaders of the Armenian Apostolic Church - Vazgen I, Garegin I and Garegin II; meetings with the spiritual leader of the Islamic Republic of Iran Ali Khamenei and the Chairman of the Council of Muslims of the

---

[*] Corresponding Author's E-mail: sergovar@gmail.com.

Caucasus Sheikh Al ul Islam Allah Shukur Pasha-Zadeh as part of the Dialogue of Civilizations.

Keywords: Georgian Orthodox Church, Ilia II, Pope John Paul II, Francis, Catholicos Vazgen I, Garegin II, multi-confessional world, Islamic Republic of Iran, Ali Khamenei, Pasha Zadeh

INTRODUCTION

Georgia has always been in the center of special attention because of its geo-strategic location. Numerous empires and religions clashed with each other at its borders. In this situation both its secular and spiritual leaders needed great wisdom, flexibility, and filigree action to take into consideration the complex reality, and to preserve and develop the unique national culture, traditions, and Orthodox religion.

Since the first days of his enthronement, Catholicos-Patriarch of All Georgia Ilia II was well aware of all this and actively began to revive this mission. The first concern of his Holiness was the settlement of relations with local Orthodox churches and the establishment of good relations with non Orthodox Christian confessions.

During the Soviet epoch, the Georgian Orthodox Apostolic Church tried to deepen the relations with local Orthodox Churches at the forums held under the aegis of the World Council of Churches, to conduct dialogue with the leaders of different religious confessions. Though, it was not an easy affair. Before the 1970s, the Georgian Church was visited by Patriarchs of Russia - Aleksey I, Pimen and Aleksey II, the Patriarch of Bulgaria Maxim, the Pope and Patriarch of Alexandria Nicholas VI, and the Catholicos of All Armenians Vazgen I. After the enthronement of His Holiness and Beatitude Ilia II, the leaders of the Churches of Constantinople, Alexandria, Jerusalem, Russia, Bulgaria, Greece, Cyprus, Romania, Serbia, Czech Republic and Slovakia, Poland, America, and Canada visited Georgia at the invitation of His Holiness.

Official visits of His Holiness and Beatitude Ilia II to local Orthodox churches were also of great interest. Those visits facilitated the recognition of the historical autocephaly of the Georgian Orthodox Apostolic Church by the Ecumenical Patriarchate of Constantinople on March 4, 1990.

The Ecumenical Patriarch, His All Holiness Bartholomew expressed well the attitude of the Orthodox world towards his Holiness Ilia II: "The fruits of your work, sacrificed to the church, are visible and bright, they will be written in golden letters by future generations on the blood-washed pages of Georgian history, just as your name is written in golden letters in our hearts" [1].

His Holiness and Beatitude Ilia II is highly respected in the multi-confessional world as a prominent religious leader. On June 5-6, 1980, His Holiness and Beatitude Ilia II was visiting the Vatican and met Pope John-Paul II. In 1997 the Pope of Rome visited Georgia. In a joint communiqué, both heads of the Church declared: "We are in the Caucasus, in Georgia, in a region of particular geopolitical and historical significance linking European and Asian, Western and Eastern cultures. The situation in this region like in other countries of the world is very tense today. At this crucial stage the world is obliged to mobilize its religious, intellectual, and physical forces to avoid global disaster" [2].

The new Pope of Rome, Francis, on behalf of the 1.3 billion Catholics, evaluated Georgia and the leader of her Church during his visit in 2016 with the following words: "I have encountered two surprises in Georgia. First is Georgia itself, I have never imagined such a place full of Christian faith. My second discovery was the Patriarch of Georgia, with his strongest and deepest faith. He is a man of God. I was shocked by his acquaintance and I had this feeling at every meeting with him. I left him with the feeling that I had found a real man of God."

Catholicos-Patriarch, His Holiness and Beatitude Ilia II attaches great importance to relations with the Armenian Church. He often stood up for Armenians in difficult conditions. These are the words written by K. Ovsepian, an Armenian from Akhalkalaki, to him: "I dare to thank you, the great Patriarch of Georgia. The Armenian people will never forget your sympathy, full of great human and civil love" [3].

His Holiness and Beatitude has met the head of the Anglican Church, the Archbishop of Canterbury, the Patriarch of the Coptic Orthodox Church of Egypt Shenouda III, the monophysite Catholicos of India of Malankara Baselios Mar Thoma Mathews I, the monophysite Patriarch of Ethiopia Abuna Tekle Haymanot, the Patriarch of Syria Jacobites Ignatius Jacob III, and the monophysite Patriarch of the East Maxim V many times.

His Holiness and Beatitude, Ilia II has surprisingly warm and direct relations with the Israeli people, which began in 1980 when the Patriarch visited Israel. The Orthodox Patriarch was met with a great ovation by Jews who had left Georgia. "No country can compare with Georgia in terms of its warm, friendly relations with Jews," said the Israeli Minister of Religion of Israel, "There has not been any misunderstanding in these relations for centuries" [4].

Our Patriarch also attaches great importance to relations with countries and their spiritual leaders. His Holiness considers that "we must learn from one another, but we must not forget our own. Real culture is a culture that unites, it is harmless and doesn't offend the cultures of other countries, on the contrary, it enriches them. It is unacceptable for any culture to become locked in itself, in its shell" [5].

In 2001, within the framework of a dialogue of civilizations, he met the Supreme Spiritual Leader of the Islamic Republic of Iran Ali Khamenei and the President of the Islamic Republic of Iran Hatami in Tehran. At the meeting with Khamenei, the Patriarch stated: "I think that the religious leaders of our countries, our governments, and societies are ready and able to respect each other and coexist in peace despite religious differences and confrontations in the past" [6].

In this turbulent 21st century, conflicts and confrontations take place mainly under the sign of religion. In such a situation, our wise and even-tempered Patriarch is faithful to peace and goodwill among people in the multi-confessional world.

REFERENCES

[1] *Proceedings of the Patriarchate*, 2016, #780.
[2] Archive of the Patriarchate, doc. #16469.
[3] *Journal "Cross of Vines,"* Tbilisi, 1978, #1, p. 15.
[4] *Journal "Cross of Vines,"* Tbilisi, 1981, #2, p. 17.
[5] *Proceedings of the Patriarchate*, 2004, October 24.
[6] *"Patriarch,"* edited by Mzia Katsadze, Tbilisi, 2006, p. 286.

In: Religion and Public Life
Editor: David Muskhelishvili
ISBN: 978-1-53618-904-9
© 2021 Nova Science Publishers, Inc.

Chapter 17

THE 'GOOD SHEPHERD' AND A STUBBORN PARISH

Alexander Daushvili[*], *Professor*
International Centre for Christian Studies at the
Orthodox Church of Georgia, Tbilisi, Georgia
Centre for Historical, Ethnological and Religious Study
and Propaganda, Tbilisi, Georgia

ABSTRACT

From this chapter a reader learns much about the 40-year priesthood period of the Catholicos-Patriarch of Georgia Ilia II, the long historical process of his relationship with the parish, his activity in the atheist state and the specific methods and means used by the Patriarch in the revival process of national consciousness and Christian values.

Showing examples, the chapter proves that during a long period of history, when the parish demonstrated "stubbornness," did not listen to the wise admonition of the Catholicos-Patriarch and made a different choice (the tragedy of April 9, the war in Tbilisi, etc.), there happened irreparable mistakes, epoch-making flaws and shed blood in the history of Georgia.

---

[*] Corresponding Author's E-mail: adaushvili@yahoo.com.

In recent years, when radical social changes, the civil war and Russian intervention have created serious problems for the parish of the Georgian Orthodox Church, the wise words and dispensation of His Holiness and his huge effort to strengthen the spiritual life of the parish, clearly leaves a positive mark on the spiritual and moral life of the Georgian population.

Keywords: Christianity, Orthodoxy, Patriarch, Georgia, morality, spirituality, faith, parish, modernity

The twentieth century turned out to be very rich in dramatic and controversial events for Georgia: a double change of the social-economic development, cultivation of a totalitarian ideology, the destructive results of militant atheism, etc. The evolution of Georgian society and its introduction to democratic values were connected with the greatest cataclysms.

The history of the Georgian Apostolic Church is equally dramatic: deprived of rights and the autocephaly by the Tsarist Synod still in 19th century and repressed by militant atheism and communist state later on, it found itself in an extremely difficult situation, in the conditions of a communist dictatorship. There was such an impression that after the so-called "Sunny Night" (as Catholicos-Patriarch Ilia II calls this period) the down would never come.

In such circumstances, in 1977, Catholicos-Patriarch Ilia II - in worldly life, Irakli Shiolashvili - became the helmsman of the Georgian Apostolic Church. His first works as Patriarch - epistles, sermons, public speeches, meetings with the representatives of society - clearly indicate that the young Patriarch tried to carefully study the situation extant in Georgia during the early 1970s, and checked up on the communist leadership of Georgia. As it turned out, the new Patriarch really wanted to find such social forces in Georgian society, through which it would be possible to save and preserve the vital energy that still existed in the Georgian Church, and then, in the second stage, to develop and broaden them for the benefit of the Georgian nation.

The first task proved to be particularly difficult - militant atheism was dominant in Georgia everywhere and in everything, and the opportunities of the Georgian Apostolic Church were very limited: It did not have property, could not use paper-based and electronic means of communication. The press, radio, and television were completely usurped by the communist party, and, besides, these were frightened and "impregnated" with atheistic ideas. In Georgia, the population was estranged from the Church. Only a small group of faithful and deeply religious people was by the side of the Georgian Patriarch. Ilia II decided to increase their number up to tens and hundreds of thousands. He singled out two social forces in Georgian society - the youth and the intelligentsia - and focused on them. The Patriarch wrote at that time: "We cannot blame the modern youth for indifference. It is a thinking, aspiring, talented youth. Its drive, ability to make a sacrifice, strive for knowledge - everything speaks of the strength and greatness of its spirit."[1]

The Catholicos-Patriarch drew attention to the positive characteristics of Georgian youth in his subsequent epistles as well, showing that His Holiness was not only interested in the problems of Georgian youth, but was also well versed in matters relating to its social development. Patriarch Ilia II acquired this knowledge by means of systematic meetings with representatives of the youth and during those special sermons when he entered into direct contact with them. These sermons were attended by such a large number of young people that the Communist authorities of Georgia even strictly warned the head of the Georgian Church.

The question of a relationship with the Georgian intelligentsia was even more complicated. An overwhelming majority of Georgian scientists were drawn to communist positions and make atheism their main worldview by the Soviet system. The young Patriarch methodically began to work with the intelligentsia. He wrote: "The intelligentsia should help people in being cognizant of the truth, but how it will be able to do so, if

---

[1] Catholicos-Patriarch of all Georgia, the Archbishop of Mtskheta-Tbilisi, Ilia II, Epistles, Vol. I, Tbilisi, 2009, p. 41.

itself is torn away from the source of wisdom - the Church."[2] Initially, only a small group of Georgian intelligentsia took the side of the Patriarch, and it was then that the Patriarch decided to restore the bridge between the Georgian Church and Georgian scientists, artificially destroyed by atheists. He created civil scientific institutions in parallel with theological academies and seminaries. Today Gelati Academy of Sciences, Saint Andrew the First-Called Georgian University and the International Centre for Christian Studies occupy a special place among such institutions.

At the beginning of his creative work, particularly during the hard years, the content of the Patriarch's epistles is mainly of a theological, didactic character. He had sensed those problems which had arisen as a result of the longstanding domination of atheism in Georgia, and in order to overcome them, he set himself the goal to popularize the national history together with theological ideas among the broad masses. The fact that the Patriarch especially emphasized one very important detail from the biography of Great Tamar in his Easter epistle in 1983 (and repeated in 1984) was not accidental: "During the period of hard trial, at the time of enemy aggression, St. Queen Tamar always took her troops to the cathedral before a battle (emphasis by me - A. D.); here the soldiers prayed together with the Queen (emphasis by me - A. D.), confessed, took Communion, and only after that attacked the enemy."[3]

By reminding them of history, the Catholicos-Patriarch attracted the attention of the parish to the role and significance of the Church, and in our supposition, already then he was preparing them for future battles...

It is not happenstance that in the Easter epistle of 1987, the Georgian Patriarch generally speaks on the vitality of the Church, accentuates its essence, significance, structure, diversity of activities and especially focuses people's attention on this issue. Eleven pages of this very special epistle are dedicated to the characterization of the essence of the Church and it is distinguished by its detail. In our opinion, it is obvious, that already in communist reality, the Patriarch had seriously warned his parish,

---

[2] Catholicos-Patriarch of all Georgia, the Archbishop of Mtskheta-Tbilisi, Ilia II, Epistles, Vol. I, Tbilisi, 2009, p. 337.
[3] Catholicos-Patriarch of all Georgia, the Archbishop of Mtskheta-Tbilisi, Ilia II, Epistles, Vol. I, Tbilisi, 2009, p. 116, p. 136.

called them to vigilance, given them important landmarks, supported them, and shown them the way to the future. We think he had already noticed in 1987 what would develop in Georgia in the 1990s and that it might result in great sacrifices. That is why he urged the people: "Only the Church is capable of our spiritual transfiguration."[4]

The fact is that the country was brought to a catastrophe by the communist leaders of Moscow. Georgia faced disintegration, clearly demanded some drastic changes and, in the opinion of the Catholicos-Patriarch of Georgia, spiritual transfiguration and being an ordinary man in such an uncertain situation would be possible only in the bosom of the Georgian Church. That is why he often called the nation to vigilance and caution - anything could happen.

Unfortunately, the Georgian population was intoxicated by the drug of atheism, even those who considered themselves to be true Orthodox, and did not listen to the exhortations of the Patriarch. This stubbornness, this obstinacy were clearly manifested on the night of April 9, when the Catholicos-Patriarch came to the rally at four o'clock in the morning to prevent the development of tragic events. This is what a historian writes: "He came to the people at the meeting late at night, told them what danger awaited them, asked them to stop the hunger strike and move with him to Kashveti Church to pray to God."[5]

Some of the historians and meeting participants share the idea that the Catholicos urged people to disperse,[6] but we suppose that the offer of general prayer in Kashveti Church was the desire to restore the historical tradition of Great Tamar. The Patriarch so persistently reminded his parish of this historical fact because he thought that Georgia stood at a historical crossroads where a difficult battle for freedom and independence awaited it, so this great thing, according to Tamar's tradition, had to be started with a prayer for the glory of the Lord.

Unfortunately, organizers and people taking part in the rally could not understand the wisdom of the Patriarch's speech, having stubbornly

---

[4] Catholicos-Patriarch of all Georgia, the Archbishop of Mtskheta-Tbilisi, Ilia II, Epistles, Vol. I, Tbilisi, 2009, p. 21.
[5] G. Mchedlishvili, History Without Distance, Kutaisi, 1999, p. 168.
[6] His Holiness and Beatitude Ilia II, 2011, Christmas Epistle, pp. 4-5.

believed that fighting the Russian military with bare hands and making sacrifices would be more proper than to offer up a joint prayer for the glory of the Lord.

The Soviet army staged a terrible carnage in the streets of Tbilisi, there were victims, Tbilisi mourned, but despite the heroic excitement, the results were more dramatic than the leaders of national movement had expected. That is why His Holiness repeatedly remembered and said later: "We could have avoided April 9." We believe that it is a true opinion, as the blood which was so tragically spilled on April 9, has followed Georgia for a long time: failure followed a failure, the number of victims grew, and the process of renewing the country dragged on.

Unfortunately, the unbalanced nature of some political leaders of Georgia helped to prepare a civil war that could not be avoided even by the efforts of the helmsman of the Georgian Church. Afterwards, the Patriarch said in his epistle with regret: "A very deplorable fact happened in Georgian history: the nation was divided. The people have opposed each other in cities and villages, at work; generations and members of families confronted each other. Such a situation has affected the psyche of people so much that they have become easily controllable byexcited and impure force (emphasis by me - A. D.)." In our opinion, such a difficult situation was caused precisely by the fact that one part of the national movement and Georgian society did not listen to the wise advice of the Patriarch.

What were the motives of these people?

The Catholicos-Patriarch found an explanation for this phenomenon as well. It is not by chance that he mentions arrogance as a particularly evil sin in his early epistles, which gnaws a person from within. Almost every year he reminded his parish of the viciousness of this pernicious disease and demanded its eradication, but the stubborn flock was not freed from this malicious disease, thus making the Patriarch say the following: "Arrogance is the first, the greatest, and the most terrible sin, which is more or less rooted in almost every person, and this is precisely the reason that prevents our approach to God ... What determines its particularity? First of all, it gives birth to all other abominations... It can set a trap for us always and everywhere and dispel the grace obtained by our many years of work, in an instant."[7]

The Georgian Apostolic Church and its helmsman, Ilia II, took upon themselves the burden of saving the nation and supported the "almost destroyed building" with their shoulders. In the conditions of the greatest historical trial of the Georgian people, the greatest authority and spiritual power of the Patriarch and the purity and morale of the Georgian Apostolic Church became the main and almost only moral supports that somehow stopped the destruction artificially induced by immature politicians. The Georgian people saw this quite clearly and that is why a majority of them unanimously gave a preference to His Holiness Ilia II over other political or public figures according to the results of some social surveys.

Georgia's independence turned out to be even more difficult and full of problems than expected: the civil war was followed by ethno-political conflicts, military clashes with Russia, the politically or economically hasty steps of irresponsible politicians, the complete impoverishment of population - and all this created a sense of hopelessness.

Before his enthronement, the Holy Synod only had 7 members. There were 34 functioning churches and 4 monasteries, as well as 15 dioceses, of which only six had a bishop in subordination to His Holiness Ilia II. The Church had only one seminary, a small circulation journal "Jvari vazisa" ("The Vine Cross") and so on. Patriarch Ilia's epistles were published in small numbers. The Church was fully provided with its own flock. In such a situation, the Patriarch of Georgia started a struggle for the spiritual recovery of Georgians: the movement for the restoration and renovation of Georgia started with his call, "Georgians, together towards God!" It was just this organization, with its strong spirituality, which tried to take the parish out of the depressing nightmare of the "Sunny Night" onto the road leading to God. His Holiness and the Georgian Apostolic Church took upon themselves the full burden of this hard work.

Very soon it became clear that the new economic system introduced in Georgia was very hard, with poor results and serious problems: It was followed by poverty and a Georgian domestic crisis... Many Georgians

---

[7] Sunny Night, Tbilisi, 2008, p. 43.

were forced to move abroad because of these problems. Serious problems emerged among the Georgian youth. The initial accumulation of capital very soon revealed some well-forgotten human traits: "arrogance, laziness, despair, debauchery, stinginess, hatred, rancor, condemnation... they alienate us from God and violate the inner harmony of our soul," His Holiness wrote at that time.[8]

The Catholicos-Patriarch prepared his flock and the nation for new challenges on the road to renewal. His epistles were more businesslike, sharp and saturated with the demands of the new time. His every word, every phrase were dictated with utmost responsibility and aimed at protecting, preserving and restoring the traditional values of Georgia. The Patriarch's following suggestion again sounds as a wise warning: "Neither only the West, nor only the East... the West is a world where everything is permitted and where violence prevails. It is strong financially, but poor spiritually, as money is idolized there... the East is also strange for us spiritually. Our grief and happiness do not correspond to their way of thinking." This admonition clearly shows the desire to bring to the forefront the basic political axiom of our historical past - a balance in foreign politics has always been the important means of survival and development for Georgia, a country surrounded by strong regional, political players.

But some representatives of the obstinate Georgian society never listened to the Patriarch's suggestions and that is why in August 2008 they had not only failed to take into account the Patriarch's advice, but also ignored the councils of American and European friends, and, as a result, everything ended tragically for Georgia. After the disgracefully lost, fatal war, the transportation of the corpses of Georgian soldiers and paying tribute to their memory became possible again thanks to the energetic efforts and authority of the Catholicos-Patriarch.

In recent years the Catholicos-Patriarch of Georgia has been very strict in his assessments of the events taking place in Georgia; he is not shy of the political leadership of Georgia and criticizes it quite sharply, when

---

[8] Catholicos-Patriarch of all Georgia, the Archbishop of Mtskheta-Tbilisi, Ilia II, Epistles, Vol. II, Tbilisi, 2009, p. 104.

necessary. In his Easter epistle of 2011, His Holiness, upset with the moral, psychological, socio-economic, and political situation in Georgia, said quite strictly the following: "There are also some non-Christian hierarchic relations that St. Maximus the Confessor called tyranny. They are based on the domination and violence of superiors and the slavish positions of inferiors. Unfortunately, non-Christian relationships prevail around us."[9]

According to His Holiness, there is only one way out of such a non-Christian state - consistent religiosity, true faith, sincerity and justice, and love for God and the nation.

The Catholicos-Patriarch's merit is enormous - the official confirmation of the autocephaly of the Georgian Apostolic Church by the Ecumenical Patriarch (1990), a constitutional agreement (concordat) between the Church and the state (2002), an increase in the number of dioceses, the restoration of the Gelati Academy of Sciences, the foundation of Tbilisi Theological Academy, the development of a dense network of universities, educational centers, and schools at the Patriarchate, an unimaginable increase in the number of believers (according to the 2014 census, 82% of population of Georgia is Orthodox), and the building of hundreds and thousands of churches and monasteries...

The Catholicos-Patriarch of Georgia assesses everything in a positive manner: "Numerous churches have been built, and they are full of people, the overwhelming majority of the population considers themselves to be Orthodox. There are no such processes in other countries, but they still live better than we do."[10]

But the Catholicos-Patriarch wishes his flock to be more perfect. He rightly says: "Each of us (I mean only believers, including clergymen) should look into his soul and assess his attitudes and feelings with impartiality. I think there are few where the Lord reigns in their heart. The greater part glorifies God only in word and only partially with deeds and does not fully rely on God."[11]

---

[9] His Holiness and Beatitude Ilia II, 2011, Easter Epistle, p. 9.
[10] His Holiness and Beatitude Ilia II, 2011, Easter Epistle, p. 8.
[11] Ibid., p. 8.

His Holiness sees a way out well and generously offers it to his flock: "Of course, people are not able to free themselves from atheistic thought so quickly... but the time has already come to correct the main spiritual landmarks; if it does not happen as so, all our efforts, our supplication will be in vain, as a prayer said incorrectly will be dispersed in the air and will not yield any result. Our life, our work, even a thought and a sense should be permeated with God and we should always look up to Him. Such an attitude is vitally necessary for everybody.

Only in this case will we be able to protect ourselves from sin and approach the condition before the Fall that was between our Creator and our primogenitors - let us swim in the ocean of love for God and be filled with His grace and mercy."[12]

Thus, the landmark has been determined and the goals have been defined. We cannot add anything to these words of His Holiness.

REFERENCES

[1] *Catholicos-Patriarch of all Georgia, the Archbishop of Mtskheta-Tbilisi, Ilia II, Epistles, Vol. I*, Tbilisi, 2009, p. 41.
[2] *Catholicos-Patriarch of all Georgia, the Archbishop of Mtskheta-Tbilisi, Ilia II, Epistles, Vol. I*, Tbilisi, 2009, p. 337.
[3] *Catholicos-Patriarch of all Georgia, the Archbishop of Mtskheta-Tbilisi, Ilia II, Epistles, Vol. I*, Tbilisi, 2009, p. 116, p. 136.
[4] *Catholicos-Patriarch of all Georgia, the Archbishop of Mtskheta-Tbilisi, Ilia II, Epistles, Vol. I*, Tbilisi, 2009, p. 21.
[5] Mchedlishvili, G., *History without Distance*, Kutaisi, 1999, p. 168.
[6] His Holiness and Beatitude Ilia II, 2011, *Christmas Epistle*, pp. 4-5.
[7] *Sunny Night*, Tbilisi, 2008, p. 43.
[8] *Catholicos-Patriarch of all Georgia, the Archbishop of Mtskheta-Tbilisi, Ilia II, Epistles, Vol. II*, Tbilisi, 2009, p. 104

---

[12] Ibid., p. 9.

[9]   His Holiness and Beatitude Ilia II, 2011, *Easter Epistle*, p. 9.
[10] His Holiness and Beatitude Ilia II, 2011, *Easter Epistle*, p. 8.

ABOUT THE EDITOR

David Muskhelishvili (October 19, 1928, Tbilisi) is a Georgian historian, Doctor of History, Academician. In 1956-1960 he was a junior researcher at Ivane Javakhishvili Institute of History, since 1960 - a senior researcher, since 1967 - Head of the Department of Historical Geography of the same institute. In 1999-2006 he was the Director of Ivane Javakhishvili Institute of History and Ethnology. Since 2001 he has been the Chairman of the Board of the International Center for Christian Studies at the Georgian Orthodox Church. Since 2006 David Muskhelishvili has been the Chairman of the Board of the Center for the Study of History, Ethnology, Religion and Propaganda. Since 2007 he has been the Chairman of the Commission on History, Archeology and Ethnology of the Georgian National Academy of Sciences.

INDEX

A

Abkhazia, vii, xv, 3, 6, 113, 129, 130, 138
abolition of autocephaly, 2, 5
academy, xv, xxv, xxvi, xxvii, xxviii, xxix, 1, 25, 35, 73, 80, 109, 130, 132, 135, 139, 140, 142, 143, 144, 156, 161, 165
acknowledgement of autocephaly, 88
acquisition of knowledge, 69
age, ix, xii, 8, 45, 49, 51, 68
aggression, xviii, xix, 102, 156
anagogical, 28, 30
ancestors, xix, xxi, xxiii
ancient world, 31, 32
antithesis, 65, 69
apostolic, v, x, xii, xiv, xvi, xxiv, xxv, xxix, 1, 2, 3, 4, 6, 7, 8, 9, 45, 109, 110, 134, 140, 147, 148, 149, 154, 155, 159, 161
Archbishop of Mtskheta-Tbilisi, vii, xv, 74, 82, 85, 129, 130, 138, 155, 156, 157, 160, 162
Aristotle, 30, 31, 32, 34, 49
Armenians, 3, 80, 94, 148, 149
atheists, 122, 156
atmosphere, xxx, 60, 101, 124

attitudes, 23, 100, 161
authority, 2, 29, 32, 68, 115, 136, 144, 159, 160
autocephaly, v, vi, x, xiii, xiv, xx, xxi, xxii, xxiii, xxiv, xxv, xxvi, 1, 2, 3, 4, 5, 6, 8, 9, 10, 73, 74, 75, 76, 77, 79, 80, 82, 84, 85, 86, 87, 88, 89, 90, 91, 92, 93, 94, 95, 98, 109, 110, 111, 112, 114, 115, 117, 119, 120, 121, 122, 123, 124, 125, 126, 137, 149, 154, 161
Azerbaijan, xxix, xxx

B

behavioral manifestations, 23
Bible, ix, xiii, 29, 55, 59, 61, 132, 141
bishop, vii, xvii, xx, xxi, xxii, xxiv, 4, 5, 6, 7, 8, 22, 52, 60, 74, 75, 80, 81, 83, 85, 89, 96, 111, 114, 121, 129, 130, 138, 159
blood, xvi, 149, 153, 158
Buddhism, xii, 28
Bulgaria, 114, 115, 148

C

capital punishment, 134
Catholic Church, xii, xvi, 27, 33, 36, 147
Catholicos Vazgen I, 148
Catholicos-Patriarch, vii, ix, x, xiii, xv, xvi, xvii, xx, xxi, xxiii, xxiv, 1, 2, 3, 4, 5, 6, 7, 8, 9, 10, 12, 16, 20, 25, 74, 75, 78, 79, 83, 84, 85, 87, 88, 91, 92, 95, 120, 121, 125, 126, 129, 130, 131, 132, 133, 134, 135, 136, 137, 138, 139, 143, 144, 147, 148, 149, 153,154, 155, 156, 157, 158, 160, 161, 162
Catholicos-Patriarch of all Georgia, xxiii, xxiv, 4, 9, 12, 20, 25, 85, 91, 138, 155, 156, 157, 160, 162
Caucasus, xvi, xxix, 3, 76, 81, 82, 84, 85, 86, 89, 90, 107, 120, 148, 149
causality, 28, 30, 41, 67
challenges, xvii, xxiv, 52, 94, 101, 160
charitable organizations, 132
children, 49, 50, 57, 64, 92, 131, 132
Christian symbol, 105
Christianity, x, xii, xxviii, 2, 3, 11, 12, 21, 27, 28, 31, 34, 36, 37, 47, 56, 57, 58, 59, 60, 62, 89, 110, 154
Christians, xxv, 33, 34, 50, 56, 58, 60, 61, 94
church, v, ix, x, xii, xiii, xiv, xvi, xvii, xviii, xx, xxi, xxii, xxiii, xxiv, xxv, xxvi, xxviii, xxix, 1, 2, 3, 4, 5, 6, 7, 8, 9, 10, 13, 27, 28, 30, 31, 32, 36, 37, 42, 46, 48, 49, 50, 51, 53, 54, 57, 58, 62, 73, 74, 75, 76, 77, 78, 80, 81, 82, 83, 84, 85, 86, 87, 88, 89, 90, 91, 92, 93, 94, 95, 98, 109, 110, 111, 112, 114, 115, 116, 119, 120, 121, 122, 123, 124, 125, 126, 131, 132, 133, 134, 135, 136, 140, 141, 142, 143, 147, 148, 149, 150, 153, 154, 155, 156, 157, 159, 161
circulation, 101, 159

cities, xiv, 102, 109, 122, 133, 158
civil law, 83
civil society, xxv, xxvi
civil war, xvi, 154, 158, 159
civilization, xix, 12, 16, 28, 47, 56
cognition, 21, 22, 52, 59
common sense, 48, 64
communication, 6, 48, 66, 85, 86
compatibility, xiii, 55, 56, 57, 59, 60, 62
compatibility of religious and secular subjects., 56
conference, xx, xxi, xxii, xxiv, xxvi, xxvii, xxix, xxxi, 6, 15
confessions, xvii, xx, 148
conflict, 69, 110, 111
confrontation, 14, 58, 92, 110
conquest, 2
consciousness, xvi, xxi, xxiv, 23, 57, 64, 66, 153
consolidation, x, 1, 2, 97
construction, 135, 142
controversial, 90, 154
cooperation, xvii, xxv, xxx, 141
cultural heritage, xxviii, 135
cultural values, xxviii
culture, xx, xxvii, xxix, 3, 6, 16, 21, 22, 25, 28, 33, 47, 64, 67, 97, 99, 145, 148, 150
Cyprus, 114, 115, 148
Czech Republic, 148

D

democracy, 13, 15, 78, 84, 120, 123, 124
Democratic Party, 121, 126
destruction, xviii, xix, 92, 159
Diocese, 74, 75, 80
diplomacy, 100, 102
dissatisfaction, x, 82, 83, 84, 85
diversity, 28, 156
draft, 78, 82, 124

Index

E

Eastern Europe, 5
economic activity, 136
economic development, 154
economics, xvii, 20
education, vii, ix, xv, 25, 32, 49, 50, 57, 58, 59, 100, 101, 107, 121, 125, 131, 134, 139, 140, 141, 143, 144, 145
educational institutions, 132, 135
educational system, 57
enlightenment, xii, 45, 46, 47, 48, 50, 140, 141, 142, 144
environment, xii, xviii, 28, 33, 47, 100
eternal return of the same, 63, 69
ethno-political conflicts, 159
Europe, xii, xxx, 27, 28, 32, 34, 91, 104
evidence, xii, 35, 39, 42, 100, 113
evil, xii, xix, xxvi, 28, 33, 50, 158

F

faith, x, xii, xv, 1, 14, 15, 16, 20, 21, 22, 23, 25, 28, 29, 33, 36, 54, 57, 58, 59, 60, 113, 123, 130, 143, 149, 154, 161
families, xviii, 131, 133, 158
February revolution, x, 1, 2, 84, 122
feelings, 60, 85, 94, 123, 124, 161
financial crisis, xxviii
first and second causality, 28, 30
folklore, 102, 106
force, x, xii, xxi, xxii, 1, 23, 28, 32, 33, 34, 40, 41, 134, 158
formation, 2, 23, 47, 69, 75, 78, 84
foundations, xiii, 20, 32, 73, 83, 94, 140
Francis, xvi, 147, 148, 149
freedom, ix, xiii, xv, xix, xx, xxii, xxv, 14, 15, 47, 52, 56, 67, 70, 74, 77, 106, 120, 121, 125, 130, 157
fresco, 99, 101, 102, 103, 104, 105, 106

G

Garegin II, xvi, 147, 148
general education, 61
Georgian Church, vi, x, xiii, xiv, xxi, xxii, xxiii, 1, 2, 3, 4, 5, 6, 7, 8, 9, 10, 16, 73, 74, 75, 76, 77, 78, 80, 81, 82, 83, 84, 85, 87, 88, 89, 90, 91, 92, 93, 94, 95, 98, 99, 109, 110, 111, 112, 114, 115, 116, 117, 119, 120, 121, 134, 136, 142, 144, 148, 154, 155, 156, 157, 158
Georgian Orthodox Church, x, xiii, xvi, xx, xxi, xxii, xxix, 2, 4, 5, 6, 8, 9, 10, 77, 79, 81, 86, 87, 88, 92, 116, 130, 135, 136, 137, 148, 154, 165
Gnosticism, xii, 28, 61
God, xii, xv, xvii, xxiii, xxv, xxvi, 6, 10, 13, 14, 16, 20, 23, 27, 28, 29, 31, 33, 34, 36, 37, 38, 40, 41, 42, 47, 48, 52, 53, 56, 57, 59, 61, 65, 69, 122, 130, 131, 132, 140, 141, 142, 143, 149, 157, 158, 159, 160, 161, 162
governance, xxvi, 10, 13, 75, 82, 84
governments, 16, 75, 150
gravitational constant, 40
gravitational force, 38, 40
Greco-Alexandrian Christian School, 56
Greece, xiv, xxvii, xxviii, 8, 29, 31, 88, 89, 90, 91, 114, 148
Greeks, xxviii, 59, 90, 91, 94, 112, 114, 123, 144
Grigol, 3, 124, 125, 141

H

happiness, xxix, 46, 47, 160
heart attack, 93
Hierophany, vi, xiii, 63
higher education, 133
history, xi, xv, xvi, xix, xx, xxi, xxii, xxiii, xxiv, xxvi, xxx, 2, 5, 10, 16, 21, 27, 34,

36, 49, 51, 56, 57, 62, 67, 73, 79, 86, 90,
   94, 97, 98, 99, 100, 101, 105, 106, 107,
   108, 109, 110, 116, 117, 121, 126, 135,
   137, 139, 140, 142, 144, 145, 149, 153,
   154, 156, 157, 158, 162, 165
hope, xviii, 16, 76, 97
hopelessness, xviii, 159
human, x, xii, xxvi, 11, 12, 13, 14, 16, 22,
   23, 28, 33, 42, 47, 57, 58, 61, 64, 66, 67,
   70, 149, 160
human condition, 66, 67
human existence, 70
human nature, 13

I

ideal, xi, 13, 15, 19, 24, 32, 46, 57, 59
ideology, xxvi, 21, 99, 100, 126, 154
Ilia II, vii, ix, x, xv, xvi, xx, xxi, xxii, xxiii,
   xxv, xxvii, xxix, 2, 9, 10, 15, 16, 20, 25,
   88, 90, 95, 126, 129, 130, 131, 132, 133,
   134, 135, 136, 137, 138, 139, 142, 143,
   144, 147, 148, 149, 150, 153, 154, 155,
   156, 157, 159, 160, 161, 162, 163
illusion, xii, 28, 33, 64
independence, xiii, xv, xix, xxii, xxiii,
   xxviii, xxx, 2, 3, 4, 8, 52, 74, 80, 85, 91,
   93, 98, 120, 121, 125, 126, 137, 157, 159
institutions, xi, xix, 11, 13, 14, 33, 47, 74,
   78, 80, 83, 122, 134, 156
interim of the Patriarch, xxiv, 74
international relations, 9
international terrorism, 15
intervention, ix, xvi, 38, 40, 154
Islamic Republic of Iran, xvi, 147, 148, 150
issues, ix, xviii, xx, xxi, 5, 15, 20, 23, 33,
   46, 50, 77, 78, 80, 83, 84, 86, 88, 89,
   101, 102, 122

J

Javakhishvili, Ivane, 45, 63, 73, 106, 135
Jews, 34, 56, 136, 150

K

Kartli, x, 1, 2, 3, 74, 99, 100, 101, 102, 103,
   108, 110, 116, 117
Khamenei, Ali, xvi, 147, 148, 150
Kirion II, x, xiii, xxiii, 1, 2, 87, 91, 92, 95
knowledge, xi, xii, xxiii, xxvi, 15, 20, 21,
   22, 24, 25, 28, 29, 31, 34, 45, 46, 47, 48,
   49, 57, 58, 59, 60, 61, 65, 66, 69, 100,
   143, 155
Kutaisi, 86, 92, 109, 117, 157, 162

L

landmark, xiv, 97, 162
laws, ix, xii, 21, 22, 28, 30, 31, 33, 35, 39,
   40, 41, 42, 65, 76, 77, 78, 85
laws of nature, ix, xii, 35, 39, 40, 41, 42
leadership, 90, 91, 154
legislation, 76, 78, 82, 84, 85
liberal theology, v, xii, 35, 36, 37
liberation, xv, xxii, 119, 121, 122, 125
light, 16, 21, 23, 32, 48, 75, 103
love, xxi, 16, 33, 58, 59, 149, 161, 162

M

majority, 15, 21, 36, 94, 125, 136, 140, 155,
   159, 161
market economy, 47
mediator, xiv, 12, 16, 88
merit, xvii, xxi, xxii, xxiii, xxiv, 13, 46, 50,
   60, 130, 137, 142, 161
metahistory, 63, 70
methodology, xii, 33, 55, 59

metropolitan, v, vii, xiv, xv, 6, 7, 8, 9, 11, 48, 74, 81, 83, 85, 88, 89, 90, 91, 92, 93, 94, 113, 123, 129, 130, 138
military, 91, 103, 106, 158, 159
miracles, xii, 35, 36, 37, 38, 39, 40, 42, 43, 65
mission, ix, xiv, 91, 97, 98, 101, 102, 106, 125, 142, 148
missionary work, vii, xv, 129, 130
misunderstanding, 82, 90, 111, 115, 150
modern science, xii, 28, 32, 33
modern society, ix
monastery, xv, 5, 49, 50, 51, 52, 92, 139, 140, 141
monks, xiv, 92, 109, 112, 135, 141
Moscow, 5, 7, 10, 17, 62, 80, 85, 157
Mtskheta, xiv, 4, 6, 7, 78, 82, 85, 97, 111, 112, 114, 119, 120, 122, 129, 133, 140
Mtskhetoba, 4
multi-confessional world, vii, 147, 148,
Muslims, xvi, 34, 94, 147
mythology, xxviii

N

national character, 76, 80, 123
national culture, 148
national identity, x, xxi, 2, 16
natural philosophy, xii, 27, 28, 31, 34
natural science, 28, 32, 37, 49, 61
noumenon, xi, 20, 24

O

occultism, xii, 28, 32
orthodoxy, 17, 47, 88, 114, 154

P

pantheism, 28

parish, vii, xvi, 7, 49, 78, 82, 131, 143, 153, 154, 156, 157, 158, 159
Pasha Zadeh, 148
patriarch, x, xvi, xvii, xxi, xxii, xxvii, 2, 3, 4, 5, 6, 7, 8, 9, 10, 51, 74, 75, 82, 85, 88, 91, 92, 93, 95, 110, 111, 112, 114, 115, 131, 132, 134, 136, 140, 142, 143, 147, 148, 149, 150, 151, 153, 154, 155, 156, 157, 158, 159, 160, 161
peace, xi, xxvi, xxix, 11, 12, 13, 15, 16, 92, 150
periodicals, xv, 120, 122
personal relations, 14
personal relationship, 14
personal welfare, 124
Petritsi, Ioane, 142
phenomenon, vi, xi, xii, xiii, 20, 24, 28, 47, 60, 63, 64, 158
Philetism, 74
Plato, xii, 32, 49, 55, 57, 59, 64, 69, 70, 75, 106
policy, xxx, 80, 85, 102, 103, 104
political leaders, 158, 160
political parties, xiv, 119, 120, 121, 124
politics, 14, 20, 46, 53, 97, 99, 100, 102, 103, 104, 107, 160
polycephalon, 140, 141
Pope John Paul II, 148
population, xvi, 36, 94, 133, 136, 154, 155, 157, 159, 161
prayer, 7, 14, 92, 131, 133, 134, 157, 158, 162
prefigurative, 28, 30
President, xvii, xx, xxii, xxiv, xxv, xxvi, xxvii, xxviii, xxix, xxx, 1, 143, 150
principles, xi, xii, 19, 20, 22, 23, 28, 31, 32, 34, 58, 59, 61, 84, 85
pseudo secularism, v, xi, 11, 12, 14
public administration, 47, 48
public figures, xxiii, xxvii, 4, 122, 159
public life, xxv, xxviii, 28
public opinion, 23

R

rationalism, 45, 47
reality, vi, xi, xvii, 14, 15, 19, 20, 22, 23, 24, 31, 79, 92, 104, 112, 113, 115, 119, 148, 156
recognition, 5, 6, 9, 10, 14, 57, 76, 83, 88, 89, 94, 126, 149
regulations, 76, 77, 78, 81
religion, xi, xii, xiii, xv, xx, xxi, xxii, xxiii, xxiv, xxv, xxvi, xxvii, xxx, 2, 12, 14, 15, 17, 22, 25, 27, 28, 29, 34, 36, 43, 46, 47, 57, 58, 61, 63, 66, 70, 81, 97, 100, 110, 120, 121, 122, 131, 148, 150, 165
religiosity, x, 11, 12, 161
religious and secular discourses, ix, 45
repetitions, 65, 66, 67, 69
requirements, 10, 23, 77, 78, 82, 83, 121, 141
resolution, 46, 76, 77, 78, 79, 81, 82, 83, 84, 86, 124
restoration, x, xiii, xiv, xv, xix, xx, xxi, xxii, xxiv, xxvi, xxix, 1, 2, 4, 5, 6, 73, 74, 75, 76, 79, 80, 84, 85, 88, 89, 91, 93, 98, 100, 103, 119, 120, 122, 124, 125, 126, 135, 136, 137, 142, 159, 161
restoration of autocephaly, x, xv, xxi, xxvi, 2, 75, 80, 93, 119, 120, 122, 124, 125, 142
rights, iv, 13, 15, 75, 77, 78, 81, 85, 112, 123, 125, 154
Russia, x, xiii, xv, xxii, xxvii, xxix, 1, 2, 4, 5, 6, 17, 79, 81, 83, 84, 85, 87, 88, 90, 92, 98, 119, 122, 123, 148, 159
Russian Church, xiii, 3, 4, 5, 6, 8, 74, 77, 81, 85, 87, 88, 89, 92, 93, 98, 137

S

Saint Anthim the Iberian, vi, 45
salvation, 36, 52, 58, 140
school, vi, xii, xiii, xxvii, 7, 49, 55, 56, 57, 59, 60, 61, 62, 130, 140, 142, 143, 145, 161
science, iv, v, ix, xii, xxv, xxvi, xxvii, 1, 14, 16, 21, 22, 25, 27, 28, 29, 31, 32, 33, 34, 35, 36, 37, 38, 39, 42, 47, 80, 135
scientific knowledge, 28, 29, 34, 59
scientific theory, 30
scientism, 28
secularism, ix, x, xi, xxv, 11, 12, 13, 14, 15, 53
secularization, xv, 12, 15, 17, 46, 47, 53, 120, 121, 123
self-awareness, 125
self-control, 46
self-knowledge, 46
self-organization, 70
services, iv, 3, 6, 7, 49, 50, 131
social doctrine, 45
society, ix, x, xiv, xv, xvii, xviii, xix, xx, xxi, xxii, xxiv, xxvi, 8, 13, 16, 22, 23, 24, 78, 119, 120, 124, 130, 131, 143, 154, 155, 158, 160
sources, vi, xiv, 51, 54, 59, 82, 98, 99, 103, 104, 105, 106, 107, 109, 110, 112, 113, 114, 127, 140
speech, xxviii, xxx, 6, 122, 125, 157
spirituality, ix, x, xxv, xxvi, 16, 49, 59, 143, 154, 159
structural multidimensionality, v, xi, 19, 20, 24
structure, 5, 10, 84, 95, 115, 156
Svetitskhoveli, xiv, 4, 6, 7, 74, 97, 98, 99, 100, 101, 102, 103, 104, 105, 106, 108, 119, 122
synergy, x, 11, 12, 13
Synod, xiii, xv, xx, xxii, xxiii, 3, 4, 6, 8, 9, 74, 75, 76, 77, 81, 82, 84, 88, 89, 90, 91, 93, 95, 116, 120, 121, 122, 130, 138, 154, 159
synthesis, xi, 20, 24, 56, 57, 65, 67, 68, 69

Index

T

Tbilisi, vii, xv, xvi, xxv, xxvii, xxix, 1, 5, 10, 11, 19, 25, 27, 45, 50, 53, 55, 62, 63, 70, 71, 73, 74, 77, 78, 81, 82, 84, 85, 86, 87, 89, 92, 95, 97, 107, 108, 116, 117, 120, 121, 122, 124, 125, 126, 129, 130, 131, 132, 133, 135, 138, 139, 143, 144, 145, 147, 151, 153, 155, 156, 157, 158, 159, 160, 161, 162
territorial, 76, 77, 79, 80, 84, 123
territory, 76, 85, 110, 113
theology, xi, xii, xx, 27, 31, 36, 37, 45, 47, 48, 55, 56, 59, 60, 61, 135, 140, 143, 144
thoughts, 30, 52, 123
traditions, 9, 33, 57, 80, 98, 144, 148
translation, 48, 114, 116, 141
true secularism, xi, 12, 13, 14
Turks, xxviii, 90, 94

U

unification, 2, 13, 16, 59, 68, 100, 103, 131
universe, xii, 12, 20, 21, 22, 24, 27, 29, 31, 32, 33, 37, 47, 57, 60, 61, 64, 66
universities, xii, 27, 32, 34, 37, 143, 161

V

violence, 74, 160, 161

W

welfare, xviii, xxvi, xxx, 102
worldview, x, xi, 11, 12, 14, 15, 31, 33, 56, 155